POSTHUMOUS

a novel about the power of belief.

PAUL AERTKER

FLYING SOLO PRESS, LLC
PARIS | DENVER | LOS ANGELES

POSTHUMOUS
PAUL AERTKER

POSTHUMOUS © 2018 by Paul Aertker
All rights reserved.

Aertker, Paul
Posthumous / Paul Aertker.— 1st ed.
p. 220 cm. 12.7 x 20.32 (5x8 in) — (Posthumous)
Summary: While living in Paris, Ellie Kerr's mom penned a series of children's
stories, yet sadly died before they could be published. Twelve-year-old Ellie
decides to finish what her mom could not, but is blocked by a password on
the computer. With the help of new friends and a strong sense of belief, Ellie
sets out to crack the posthumous code and publish her mother's books.
© 2018, Paul Aertker
1. Travel—Fiction. 2. Language and languages—Fiction.3. Self-actualization
(Psychology)— Fiction. 4. Cancer (Ovarian)—Fiction. 5. Mothers
and Daughters—Fiction. 6. Fathers and Daughters—Fiction. 7. Loss
(Psychology)—Fiction. 8. Geography— Fiction. 9. Schools—Fiction. 10.
Europe—Fiction. 11. France—Fiction. 12. Paris—Fiction. I Title.

Edited by Brian Luster using the Chicago Manual of Style, 16th edition |
Cover design by Pintado | Interior design by Amy McKnight | All designs,
graphics, photographs © 2018 Paul Aertker and Flying Solo Press, LLC

ISBN-13: 978-1-940137-99-5/ ISBN-10:1-940137-99-5
eISBN 978-1-940137-00-1

Posthumous | Printed worldwide
US Copyright Information on file
Library of Congress Control Number: 2017958510

Foreword

My mom used to say,
"There's a first time for everything."

Unless of course

you die before you ever get the chance.

Like she did.

So . . .

with a little help from my dad

and my uncle,

I wrote this story—

and I'm dedicating it to my mom.

Here goes:

Dedication

To Mom—

I love you and I always will.

Together Forever

Yours truly,

Ellie-

Ella Elizabeth Kerr

Age 12 & 344/365ths

Welcome Home

At the front of our new house there was an old doormat.

It said WELCOME HOME.

I pushed the door open and stepped inside for the first time ever.

Home, I thought.

A lump in my throat sank like a giant pill I had to swallow. I turned around, looked out into the yard, and then down at the straw mat at my feet. The letters were faded and worn from wear, and, from my point of view, backward and upside down.

It looked like:

ƎWOH
ƎWOƆ˥ƎW

As I focused on the expression "welcome home" and what that really meant, I realized right there in the middle of this jumble were *M* and *O*. The two letters you needed to make the word *mom*, which must be where the word *home* came from in the first place.

Mom and *home.*

To me, those two things just go together, you know.

Three months after Mom had died, *home* was still hard for me to say.

The American movers came early that morning in a big truck, an eighteen-wheeler, and it practically took up the whole street. Music blared from a radio while two men with tattoos flung open the back doors and clanged a long metal ramp onto the concrete.

The woman in charge of the movers was smacking gum when she walked up the sidewalk to the house. The name patch on her shirt read COOKIE.

My dad came out and said hello and held the front door open for her. Cookie and Dad toured the empty house and talked about where the furniture was supposed to go.

One of the movers came in and laid rubber pads on the hardwood floors.

For the next hour or so, I stood by the front door watching the men unload our belongings.

Out in the street, a boy with spiky blond hair rode a trick bike past the house. He zigged and zagged from the curb to the sidewalk, popping wheelies over bumps in the driveways. Each time his front tire came down, he'd look up and glance over at me.

I knew exactly what he was doing. I was officially the new kid on the block, and he had come to see who I was.

A while later the boy rode by again, but this time he kept his head turned, staring and pedaling. He wasn't paying much attention to where he was going. His bike was aimed straight at the back of the movers' truck. If he kept riding, he was going to have a terrible accident. At the last second he swerved, the movers jumped out of the way, and the boy rode up the ramp and into the back of the trailer!

Cookie came running outside. "Hey, kid! Get out of there. We're moving 'em in—we aren't moving *you* out!"

She slapped her leg and started howling at her own joke, and the other movers laughed too.

I guess that's humor for moving people. It wasn't really that funny to me. I was actually worried the boy had broken some of our stuff, like my mom's picture-and-mirror collection or the laptop that held her stories.

I might not ever get my mom back, but at least I could have some of the things she cared about.

Inside the back of the truck, the boy spun his bike around and rolled down the ramp and into the street.

"Who was that?" Cookie asked.

"That was that Pete Morgan," one of the movers said. "We moved the mom and him in last year."

The other mover added, "I know you remember the mom. Over on Ash Street."

Cookie nodded. "Pete Morgan!" she yelled. "Go home to your mother!"

Pete glanced back and looked right at me.

All day long the movers shuttled back and forth from the truck to the house, sweat dripping off them. Packing paper and torn tape littered our front yard so much that you would've thought it was a recycling plant. In the grass there were a couple of dining room chairs, two tables, a collection of lampshades sitting on a piece of cardboard, and my mother's dresser.

Cookie tapped her foot on the old welcome mat. She wore long cutoff blue jeans with work boots, and her bushy blond hair stuck out of a baseball cap that was backward on her head. I peeked over her clipboard, and she stopped smacking her gum to look at me.

"Moving back to America all the way from Paris, France?" she said. "Now that there's a *long* move in my book!"

I didn't say anything. Mom used to say, "People are strange." She was quoting a Jim Morrison song she liked. But she was right—most people are strange.

After a while I got bored watching furniture pile up in the front yard. There was nothing to do, and I missed my friends from Paris. So I went inside, into my house, to my new bedroom with nothing in it except a mattress with no sheets and a blinding light bulb on a lamp with no shade. No pictures, no stuffed animals, no posters. Nothing.

It was a big white room that felt empty, just like I felt without Mom around. I dove onto the mattress and stared at the cardboard boxes.

Dad called out. "Ellie!" he yelled, his voice echoing against the blank walls. "Come see this!"

I sprang off the bed and ran down the hall, hopping over a stack of folded moving blankets. "I'm coming."

Dad was on the floor in the master bedroom, sitting in a nest of plastic shrink-wrap.

He pulled a laptop out of a box. "Look! Here's Mom's computer that you were looking for."

"Yes!" I said. "We've still got her stories!"

He handed me the laptop and the power cord. "Remember, you have to take off the little European adapter first, sweetie."

The Europlug made me think about how fantastic our life in France had been and how quickly everything had ended. We had lived in Paris for years, and while we were there, my mother had written a series of stories called Explore the World. I had read them all because they were the best.

Mom said I was "biased," which meant it wasn't fair for me to judge her books.

Hello! Of course I was biased. She was my mom!

She also said they weren't books but manuscripts. "Books are published," she used to say. She never got her books published, and it wasn't from *not* trying, either. She had written letters and sent books—I mean manuscripts—to publishers all over the world: in the US, in Australia, and in the UK. They had rejected my mother's stories so many times that she thought about writing a book about rejection letters. Before she could get around to writing that book, she died.

I removed the adapter thingy from the cord, plugged the computer in, and waited for the laptop to boot up. I was so excited. At least I could read my mom's stories. Not that that would ever replace her. But still, it was something.

Dad showed me a stack of papers. "Look at these rejection letters. Incredible!"

"What?" I said. "How many rejection letters she got?"

"Yeah," Dad said. "And they all say basically the same thing. 'Dear Author, We have to be very selective . . .' blah blah."

"Hey, Dad. Remember that rejection Mom got the day we went to the Eiffel Tower?"

"Huh?" Dad said. He had already gone into reading more of Mom's papers. Since Mom had died, Dad had been in this fog, so that he never got too happy or too sad over anything. He and Mom were best friends, and they used to run every day, and Dad would say he was going to live longer than anyone. But ever since Mom died, he hadn't mentioned this anymore.

And that scared me. A lot.

"You remember," I said. "The email from the editor in England that instead of writing to Mom as 'Dear Etta,' the woman wrote 'Dear Sarah'?"

"Oh yeah!" Dad said with a half smile. "Didn't Mom write her back?"

"I did," I explained. "Mom told *me* to. I didn't like

it that she called someone Sarah whose name was actually Etta."

From outside there came another loud sound of the metal ramp hitting concrete. Then Cookie and the other movers burst out laughing.

Dad looked at me. "So . . . what did you end up doing?"

"Mom told me that agents and editors were busy. She said the person might have just made a mistake."

"Your mom was wonderful."

I looked back at the computer screen. It was taking forever to load.

"Hey, Dad, this is kind of random, but, um, do you think I could publish Mom's books even though she's not . . . I mean, do you have to be alive to publish something?"

"It's done all the time," he said, putting a box on the floor. "There're plenty of writers, artists, even business guys, who don't get recognized for what they've done until they're gone. Van Gogh died poor, without a franc to his name, and now more than a hundred years after his death his paintings sell for millions."

"Really?"

Dad grabbed another stack of papers. "Some things don't make it for a reason, though. I'm not in the book business, and given her track record with editors and agents, it seemed no one wanted to publish your mom's stories."

"I'll show them," I said. "I'll print up the whole

series and give it to my friends, and they'll like it. I know they will. Then I'll tell the publishers, and we'll start printing the books."

He touched my shoulder. "Ellie, I'm so sorry."

"Huh?" I said, looking up from the laptop.

"I'm sorry about Mom," he said. "I miss her too."

"Yeah, Dad, I know you're sorry. You've told me about a million times."

He stared at the ceiling. "I know. It's all I know to say. I'm just trying to make sense of everything that has happened to our family. So at least I can say I'm sorry."

"Me too." I bit my lip. "Me too, Dad."

"You do what you need to do with those stories," he said. "And if showing Mom's stories to your friends helps you deal with what you're going through, then so be it."

"You really think it's okay for me to publish them?"

"Belief makes the imagination come to life," he said as his mind drifted into a fog.

The login screen on the laptop had come up, and a cursor blinked in the password box.

There was something odd about using my mom's password now.

"Did you forget her password?" Dad asked.

"You told me the brain never forgets."

"True."

"And I've known the password since I was eight."

I typed it in: *123Iamme.*

The code was silly, like my mother. She had told me

 8

that a password should make you feel good when you type it in. That way you always start out on the right foot.

The computer made a sound. *Blip.*

The screen read THE PASSWORD IS INCORRECT.

"What's going on?" Dad said. He raised his eyebrows. "Try it again."

I clicked OK and tried the password again.

Blip.

Dad saw my frustration, and he got on all fours and curled his lips like he was pouting. He scrunched up his face and flipped his glasses upside down. It was ridiculous, and I couldn't help but giggle.

"Hmm. What's the matter with this computer?" he said, trying to be playful. "It's got an upset stomach. Is it going to start burping like your mom?"

He fake-burped.

I knew he was talking about Mom's "incident" at the Eiffel Tower. But right then I didn't want to think about the funny stories about Mom. I wanted to get the stories she had written. And they were locked in the computer.

I snapped, "The password's not working, Dad."

He fixed his glasses. "Did you put in one-two-three-I-am-me?"

"Twice."

"Give me that thing."

I handed Dad the laptop; his fingers clacked on the keyboard.

Blip.

"I don't get it," he said, looking honestly puzzled. "We've had that password for ten years—since you were two. It was one of the first things you ever said in your whole life."

"What?"

"Mom read Dr. Seuss to you, something like *Fox in Socks* or something. And you kept repeating the words, and then you made up 'One two three I am me.'"

"I'm so smart!"

"Didn't you use this computer when we were still in Paris?"

"I just told you about the email from the woman in England. And the password was one-two-three-I-am-me."

Dad tried the same password a fourth time, and then this crazy and scary-looking screen came up! I wrote down some of what I saw.

```
password = false;
            //attempts  remaining  =
0
            //Data    is    encrypted.
Target hash denied

while  ((attemptCount++  <  4)  &
(password == false))
            {
```

```
//::invalid::
        }

      << std::endl
      {
```
Error. Password is incorrect. Perma-
deletion and data destruction of
entire disk will begin in 10 seconds,
9 seconds, 8 seconds

In a split second Dad's expression flashed fear. He jammed the OFF button with his finger and left it there, killing the power. He set the laptop on the mattress and shook his head.

From his bedside table he grabbed the small wooden box that used to contain Mom's ashes, and he tapped his fingers on the top.

He mumbled to himself. "That doesn't explain why the password doesn't work."

"Maybe she changed it," I said.

"What?" Now Dad was snippy with me. "She battled cancer, and then right before she died she changed the password on her computer?" He opened his eyes wide and looked right at me. "And she didn't tell her husband of nearly fifteen years? Why didn't she tell anybody? It doesn't make sense!"

"Don't get so upset with me, Dad. It's not my fault. I didn't change it."

"I'm sorry," he said and calmed down. "You really

didn't mess with it?"

"No, Dad. I'm serious. I don't even know how to change the password, not on that homemade computer."

"If you didn't switch the password, then who did?"

I let out a frustrated sigh. "I don't know. I didn't do it. . . . Maybe Munda did?"

Munda was a woman from the French West Indies, and she was our cook in Paris who became Mom's nurse while she was sick.

"Not possible," Dad said. "That woman is a saint."

"What about Henry?" I asked. He was Dad's assistant, and they had worked side by side in our apartment in Paris. "Maybe he did something to it."

"Henry is a computer genius," Dad said. "So that's possible, but there's no logical reason he would do this."

"Why are you so freaked out?" I said. "Anybody can hack into a computer. Give it to any IT guy; give it back to Henry. He wrote the software. I bet he can break into it in about two seconds."

"Normally that's true," he admitted. "But this was one of my work computers that I backed up financial information on—like undisclosed bank accounts of royal families. So the data is encrypted."

"A computer guy couldn't figure it out?"

"Yes and no," he said. "It's protected by a secret program, like a blockchain that Henry developed just for my company. Henry used to work for the IT departments at MI6, the CIA, and the NSA. He made a code that is virtually unbreakable and the data completely inaccessible."

"Can't Henry just copy one of Al Gore's rhythms?"

"Algorithm," Dad corrected. "He built the system to prevent tampering by that kind of math program."

"But there are kids on the Internet who could hack into it."

"Yes and no," he said. "But worse than anything is that the security codes are written to destroy the data if someone tries to log on more than three consecutive times with an incorrect password. On the fourth attempt, the software thinks it's being hacked, so it begins destroying itself. The bank account numbers and your mom's stories would be corrupted. Unreadable."

"Whatever," I said. "We still have the printouts of her stories."

Dad set his glasses down on a box. "The day we went to the Eiffel Tower, your mother had Munda recycle all of the printed copies of her stories."

"Why did she do that?" I asked.

Dad shook his head. "Mom must have known she was going to die soon. But why would she change the password? Why would she want to make it difficult, if not impossible, to get into her computer, and to get to her stories? Now that, Ellie—that's a mystery."

"Maybe . . ."

"It doesn't matter, sweetie," he said, putting the

ashes box back on the bedside table. "The results are the same. Without the code, we don't have access to her stories."

"You mean," I said, "if we don't get the correct password, then we can't log on to the computer, and if we can't do that, then Mom's stories are lost forever?"

"Forever," he said. "Forever."

 14

Paris

The apartment we lived in in Paris looked out onto the Eiffel Tower.

The City of Light was a great place to live. It seemed everything was alive. And there was chocolate everywhere.

To be honest, I didn't really want to move to France, but my dad took a job there. He worked for the king of France. I know, I know—I'm almost thirteen now, and I know France doesn't have kings and queens anymore, thank you very much. But honestly, there is some French guy who lives in Spain and is the real heir to the French throne. Or so he claims. No kidding. Look it up. Dad and Henry called him "the Dauphin."

My father said the Dauphin's family might not technically be royal anymore, but they had more dough than all the baguettes in France. *Dough* was what my dad called money, and this ex-royal family had hired him to manage their secret fortune they still had in France. And that's why we moved.

Like I said, I didn't really want to go. I mean I wanted to go there and see the Eiffel Tower and all, but to live there was different. After almost eight years in the United States, in the same place and the same house, I didn't want to leave. I couldn't imagine being without my friends, especially my best friend, Vicky, who was the funniest person in the world. She cracked me up, because when she got tired of talking to you, she would text you or write little notes to you, right in the middle of a conversation. At the end of her notes, she'd put a little happy face with a cute upturned nose like hers. I know she's still my best friend, because when we moved to France, Vicky would send messages, and they ended the same way, saying we were friends forever, and then she would add little smiley faces.

My mom loved this about Vicky.

In Paris, we weren't ordinary people. Dad worked for this ex-royal family of France, and Mom was a writer, which in France is the most important job you could ever have. My mother had always written for an ad agency, and then, on the anniversary of 9/11, she began writing for kids.

We were standing near the Place de la Concorde, which is in the center of Paris. Mom and I were wearing dresses and sweaters, and Dad was wearing a blazer and tie. Across the plaza, international flags at a hotel flapped in the wind. Except the American flag. Someone had wrapped a black band around it.

I remember asking, "Why is the American flag over there like that?"

"I don't know," Mom said, shrugging. "Ask Mr. Wikipedia."

My dad knew everything.

"The flag," he said, "is wrapped *en berne*, which is the French sign of mourning and respect for the dead. It's like flying the flag half-staff. I imagine someone is doing this on September eleventh because of the terrorist attacks in 2001 in the US."

"But," Mom said. "There've been many terrorist attacks all over the world since then."

"I wasn't even born yet," I said.

"Interesting," Mom said.

She had a puzzled look on her face as she dug into her purse and typed a note into her phone.

"Yes!" she said. "If kids travel!"

"What, Mom?"

She put her hand on my head and looked toward the Eiffel Tower. "When you travel," she said, "you get a much better sense of where people are coming from. Right?"

"Right?" I said, not understanding.

"So . . . you're more likely to make a friend instead of an enemy."

"Okay . . . ," I said. "I still don't get it."

"I've got an idea for a story," she said. "No. Wait. Calvert? How many languages are there in the United Nations?"

"Hundreds," he said. "There are almost two hundred member nations in the UN, but only six official languages."

"What are the languages?" I asked.

Dad answered in alphabetic order. "Arabic, Chinese, English, French, Russian, and Spanish."

"Six stories," Mom mumbled. "A whole series."

"What, Mom?" I asked again.

"I shouldn't speak about it until I've written some of it down."

That's how my mom started writing children's books.

The other thing that made us different was that we were expats, which meant that we were people from one country living in another country. Dad had told me that expats were experts at making friends.

At my new school, ASP—the American School of Paris—I made friends quickly because most everyone else was also an expat. My parents bent over back-ward to make things right for me since we'd said good-bye to Vicky and my other friends and every-thing else I knew back in the States.

We were expats. So no one was normal.

To be honest, everything was different in Paris. Back home in the States, Vicky used to come over to my house to jump on the trampoline or go to the mall. In France, I'd meet my friends at the carousel under the Eiffel Tower.

My three best friends at ASP were from three different continents. Not countries. Not counties. Continents. Ji Yoon was my best South Korean friend. Alexa was my best South African friend. And Bella was my best Argentinean friend. Three countries. Three continents.

We were perfect for each other, except for one teeny tiny problem: there wasn't one language that we all three spoke well.

Ji Yoon, Alexa, Bella, and I met every Saturday at the Eiffel Tower. From there, one of our parents would take us to see the sights. We were like four sisters. We each had long hair. Bella and Ji Yoon had black hair, and Alexa and I had blond hair. We spoke broken English, French, and our favorite, Franglais, which was a mix of French and English.

Our very first Saturday, we went to the Louvre to see the *Mona Lisa*. We thought the painting was kind of weird-looking. But we made a game of everything. Walking around the Louvre, we would make up stories about hidden messages in the artwork.

The next Saturday, we went to another museum—the Musée d'Orsay. This time we wore berets and took sketch pads with us. We sat on a bench in front of a van Gogh painting and drew. Alexa actually sold one of her drawings to this German guy who had been watching us! With the money, she bought us chocolate croissants.

That's really how we became new best friends.

In Paris there was always something going on. On the sidewalk, in a park, or in a café. Jugglers and skaters. Crêpes and ice cream. It had everything. Did

I mention there was chocolate everywhere?

Turns out the City of Light was a great place to live. Unfortunately, it also happened to be the place where my mother would die.

Some News

Everything had been all right for a long time. By the time I turned eleven and seven-twelfths, I had learned to speak French. "*Oui, madame*, blah, blah, blah." I could actually speak another language! It was the best.

A few weeks after New Year's Day, Dad came back from a trip to the US, and he announced that he had taken another new job. We would be moving back to the States in the summer.

I didn't want to leave the new friends I had made at the American School, especially Ji Yoon, Alexa, and Bella. But I had to admit I was excited. Part of me had been itching to go back home. We would be moving to a whole new city and state, and I secretly dreamed of walking into a French class and speaking fluently with the teacher. I craved the feeling of being home, back in the USA. Not even at my old school, but just being in America. Mom, Dad, and me. At home where everything was right and nothing was wrong.

Then it happened. Mom got sick. Scary sick. It was obvious even to me. Something was seriously wrong with my mother.

This is how I found out.

A week after Dad had told us about his new job, he and I were sitting at the dinner table. Munda, our cook, was in the kitchen.

The curtains in the living room were open, and outside the window, the Eiffel Tower was lit up. Everything in the apartment was nice and neat. Since my dad would have rich people over from time to time, we always had to keep our table set for a king. It was first-class all the way. A gold chandelier hung above a red mahogany table. The silverware was real silver, and the drinking glasses were real crystal.

I can remember it perfectly, not that I want to. It was cold and a little rainy. January. I was halfway through fifth grade. I lit the candles on the table just as Mom walked down the stairs from her bedroom. And as soon as Mom sat down at the table, we knew something was up. She was always dressed nicely, but that night she was wearing running pants, and her typically perfect auburn hair was a mess.

"Ah," she moaned, holding her lower back when she sat down. "I think I pulled my back yesterday."

"On our run?" Dad asked.

"Yeah," she said. "I guess."

Dad joked. "I thought you were just a wimp."

Mom and Dad were both big runners. Sometimes when we'd go to a park, Ji Yoon, Bella, Alexa, and I would play while my parents jogged around the outside track, so they could run and talk and keep an eye on us at the same time.

Munda poked her head out of the window between the kitchen and the dining room. She was outfitted in her usual white clothing, which made her coffee-colored skin glow even more. As always, she wore a necklace. That night she sported a long golden chain studded with tiny eyes. Her hair was wrapped in a piece of orange-and-yellow fabric, but she had fixed it in such a way that it looked like a flower. Second only to my mom, she was the prettiest woman I'd ever seen. Munda came into the dining room, humming some Caribbean tune and carrying a huge platter of her famous dish of spicy chicken and bananas. It was weird but good. When she spoke, she had a funny French Creole accent, and words like *get* would sometimes sound like "git," and *think* like "tink," and *that* like "dat."

"What's getting ahold of you, woman?" Munda said to Mom as she set the platter on the table.

"My back is killing me," Mom said. "That mattress is still not right for me. I love France, but I'm not sure I like their mattresses."

"We can change it out," Dad said. "I'll call the office tomorrow and have someone bring a new one."

"Calvert!" Mom snapped. "This is already the third mattress you've had delivered. It's me. I don't think it's the mattress. It'll be all right tomorrow."

"You haven't liked a mattress in six years," Dad said. And he was right. "Ever since that little car accident."

"That was my back," Mom said.

"I think you need to get to a doctor," Munda said, walking back into the kitchen. "And that's that."

The next day, Mom didn't go to the doctor because she felt too bad. In fact, she didn't get out of bed. The following day, Munda saw to it that Mom made it to the doctor. Mom's back was a mess. She could barely walk, and when she did, she limped. So Dad called Antoine, his driver from his office.

Antoine came to the apartment, he and Munda helped Mom out the door, and they took her to the doctor.

At dinner that night, Mom came to the table, still bent over, holding her back and her stomach. Her hair was wavy but messy like she hadn't fixed it right. Even the brown in her eyes seemed cloudy.

"What did the doctor say?" Dad asked.

"She said that I either tore or pulled a ligament. But I should treat both the same way. Ice and rest."

We could hear Munda in the kitchen moaning, "Isn't a ligament."

"Dr. Munda?" Dad said, jokingly. "What is your diagnosis?"

"I don't know what it is that's getting that woman," Munda said, talking to us through the big window separating the two rooms. "Not a ligament. That's for sure."

"How do you know that?" Dad said, still teasing her. Mom wasn't talking. She took her pain pills and ate the fish and rice and peas quietly.

"Deary," Munda said. "I used to take care of a lot of women in the Caribbean. And I go with how I feel . . . and right now, I am feeling it. And that's that." That's how Munda ended any argument. When she said she felt something, she meant it. And you didn't question it again.

"How do you feel?" Dad said to Mom.

"Awful," Mom said, yawning. "Horrible. Terrible. I can't move, and the pain pills don't seem to be helping. They're just making me tired, and that's not fun either."

"What can we do for you?" Dad said.

"Nothing," Mom said, yawning again. "I'll be okay. I just need some sleep."

She was right. Two days later, Mom woke up feeling fine. But at dinner that night she couldn't eat the Cuban black beans. Another Munda specialty.

"Gosh," Mom said, standing at the table and holding her stomach. "Is it me or is it because I haven't run in almost a week that I'm getting this pooch belly. I'm fat as . . ."

"Ahem," Munda coughed. She was a lot bigger than mom. "I think that women are more beautiful when they are not all skins and bones like fashion ladies here in Paris."

"You look great, Etta," Dad said, taking off his tie. "We càn go for a run tomorrow. Let's go to the indoor track over by the American School. Maybe Ellie can have Ji Yoon meet us there. They live out by the school, don't they?"

"Yeah," I said. "And then can we go to Disneyland?"

Dad shook his head, looking at me like I was crazy, like it was a big deal to go to Disneyland, which is only one train ride away from Paris. Easy. But he answered me by saying nothing, which meant that it was too much trouble to go.

"I told you, now," Munda said from the kitchen. "Uh-huh. I know I am not a doctor."

"Not yet," interrupted Dad.

"True," Munda said. "But if I were, I'd be running tests. I've seen island women with this problem. I know it and I've seen it with my own eyes."

"We'll see about it next week," Mom said. She burped. "But I don't think I can eat black beans tonight. I've got enough gas already."

"Don't let it go in here!" Dad said, joking to Mom as she headed up the stairs. Dad tapped me on the arm, and we giggled.

When I came in from school the next day, Dad was already home from work. Not a good sign. Munda was quiet as a church mouse. Also not good.

Mom and Dad were sitting silently on the sofa in the living room.

Outside, the Eiffel Tower stood alone in the rain.

Dad was still in his business suit, and Mom was wearing nice jeans and a black long-sleeve shirt. Her hair was short and draped across her cheek. She looked so beautiful.

"Ellie," Dad said. "We have—"

"I have . . . ," Mom said, interrupting. Her voice was deep and serious. "I have some news to share with you."

The tone said it all. When people have good news, they say, "Good news!" When they have bad news, they "share it."

My backpack slid off my shoulder and onto the rug. I plopped down in the armchair across from the couch. My eyes bulged out of my head as thoughts raced through my brain looking for answers. I hadn't done anything.

Divorce! I thought. *Wait. She said, 'I have some news to share. . . .' She's leaving. Mom's leaving us.*

The cold and the clouds seeped into the room. The whole apartment—upstairs and downstairs—was silent. Except for the rain outside.

Munda had even stopped moving in the kitchen. Outside the tall windows, I could hear traffic noise coming from the streets below. A siren wailed. It was already an awful scene, and nothing had happened yet.

"Ellie," Mom said. I lifted my head and focused on her soft brown eyes. The clouds were there again. "We've always spoken to you like an adult," she said. "I guess that's part of being an only child. You get dragged along with the parents. But we have taken you to some pretty neat spots, haven't we?"

I swallowed and looked at Dad. He was staring at

Mom's profile, and the muscles in his face were tight; his lips were thin and white. Then he reached out and held Mom's hand.

"I've been practicing with Munda all day," Mom said. "I've been practicing how to tell you my news. It's hard for me to say it when I don't even believe what I am saying. I'm not making any sense, am I? I'm sorry Ellie. I don't know how to tell you this. Everything I've read tells me that I should just be honest and tell you straight."

She closed her eyes, breathed deeply, and then looked at me.

"I was at the doctor's office again today," she said. "I have cancer."

After I had heard the word *cancer*, I didn't hear much else or I didn't understand what had been said. I heard her talking about the type of cancer and the stages, the treatments, and the options.

With a desperate smile, she tried to sound upbeat as she spoke about the diagnosis and the prognosis. I didn't know the vocabulary. The words swirled around the room and in my head. She rambled on and on, saying things I didn't, couldn't comprehend.

I felt my body rise from the armchair. I had no control—as if I were floating. Somewhere in the middle of this flight, my mother caught me and wrapped her arms around me.

Like a violent storm, the tears came.

I heard Dad say something about how active Mom

was. He said something about the doctor wanting to try the biggest medicine they had since Mom was in such good shape. I listened, but I couldn't seem to hear. The voices sounded like people mumbling from the bottom of a swimming pool. The only word I really heard was *cancer*. It was like a bomb. Right on top of my head. The words clanged in my brain, and I couldn't think because I didn't believe the news. Didn't want to. My mom was funny. And cancer was not. Not at all.

My mom held me as the room spun.

This is not happening to me; I am watching a movie. That's it! This is a bad movie. Would someone please change the channel?

A Talk

The next day I was numb. My body could have slept forever. I stayed in bed and sank deep into the middle of my stuffed animals, hoping they would somehow protect me.

I shuffled downstairs in my pajamas and slippers. Dad was in his office, sitting behind a wall of computer monitors, speaking Spanish into a headset. I peeked in through the crack in the door and spied a man who had to be Henry, Dad's assistant. He was on a cell phone, speaking Arabic. Neither seemed to notice I was there.

In the living room, Mom was also on the phone, pacing. She was wearing her usual running outfit with crazy-colored running shoes. Mom circled the coffee table three times before she spotted me. Then she smiled and gave me a little wave.

Munda was in the kitchen, cooking. "Do you want your breakfast or your lunch, deary?"

"I'm not hungry," I said as I plopped down at the dining room table.

The lump in my throat was just starting to grow. I wondered if I, too, might be sick.

Mom stood behind me and ran her fingers through my hair. Goosebumps crawled up my spine. My body folded forward, and I laid my head on Mom's running gloves.

"It's one of the problems with expat life," Mom said into the phone. "We always think we'll get around to doing whatever it is we're supposed to do. I guess I was waiting until we went back to the US."

I could hear the other person's mumbled voice coming through the phone.

"You're right," Mom said. "Home is where we make it."

There was another pause.

"The problem," Mom said, "is that we've been gone too long. You know me. I'm never sick and never worry."

Mom stopped rubbing my head for a second, and she briefly left her hand in my hair.

"I know," Mom said. "I guess it's been a couple of years. Probably three. Ever since I had that car accident, which doesn't make sense. Car accidents don't give you cancer, you know."

There was another pause while the other person talked.

"I should have felt something before," Mom said. "I just blamed my problems on the accident, when it was obviously something totally unrelated."

From the kitchen, I could hear Munda putting away the dishes ever so quietly. *Clink. Clink.*

Mom walked into the living room. "I feel like I've been queasy forever," she said still on the phone, "but who isn't at this age. I can't believe this is what I am going to be doing now."

Munda put a croissant in front of me. "Our spirits are working together," she said, whispering in my ear. "We'll do what is right for your mama. You hear me now? And we follow our hearts. That's what we do."

"I will," I heard Mom say into the phone. "I just went for a run this morning, and I feel okay actually. I gotta go—my angels are here. See you tomorrow then. Bye-bye."

She hung up the phone.

"Hello, sweetie," Mom said, leaning over to give me a kiss on the cheek.

Then Mom hugged Munda for a very long time.

"What would I do without you?" Mom said.

Munda smiled and went back into the kitchen.

Mom sat down next to me. "I know this has got to be hard for you. But don't worry. I can hardly believe what's happening either."

I looked at her face and saw that she had been crying. Her eyes and her nostrils were red.

"Do you really have cancer, Mom?"

"Do I?" She paused. "No."

I looked at her like she was crazy.

"My body has cancer," she said. "*I* do not. My soul does not have cancer."

I must have looked confused.

 32

"Who we are is on the inside," she said, tapping her sternum. "This is me in here, but this body is just a body that my soul is using. Temporarily."

I understood. My mother was always spiritual, "connected to the universe," she would often say. So it wasn't odd for her to separate body and soul. Something in her smile, the way the corners of her lips drooped, something there told me she too was afraid.

"I'll be honest with you, Ellie," she said with a forced swallow. "I'm scared, and I wish I didn't have this. But the sooner I stop denying it, the sooner I can get on with fighting it."

"So you'll go to the doctor, and he'll do whatever and . . . ," I said. "And then you'll be fine?"

She bit her lip, and a single tear, one that she'd been holding back, finally spilled over and down her cheek.

"I hope so," she said. "At this point, we do what Dr. Manon says. She's top-notch—she's one of the best, not only in France but also worldwide. She used to teach at Johns Hopkins in Baltimore."

"But—"

She squeezed my right hand with both of hers, making a little sandwich. "All you need to know is that Dr. Manon is the best of the best." She paused. "I refuse to lie to you, Ellie. I have advanced ovarian cancer. It is not a good cancer to have."

"A *good* cancer?"

"You're right," she said with a small but honest grin. "There's not one that's good."

The lump grew in my throat. "Advanced sounds bad."

She patted her lips with her tips of her fingers. "What we can hope for . . . at this stage . . . is that it will go into remission for a very, very long time. Okay?"

"Mom, you can do this," I said. "You can beat cancer. People do it all the time. There are, like, thousands of people who beat cancer. Right? And you're not afraid of anything. You are the one who went looking for rats in the catacombs. Remember? You're the strongest mom in the world."

"That's sweet of you." She sniffled and grinned. "Maybe the strangest, not the strongest. People are strange, you know."

She gave me a big hug and then stood. "You're right," she said. She made a fist. "Dr. Manon said that we have to be very aggressive with the treatment. It will make me sick. So plan for that."

"Will you lose your hair?"

"Probably. We are about to go down a hard road. I can do it, but I will need your help."

"To do what?"

"Laugh with me."

"Laugh?" I asked.

"Humor is good medicine," she said. "You can hold my hand and tell me stories, funny ones. Hugs and jokes and laughs, all right?"

"Okay . . ."

Mom called toward the kitchen. "Munda?"

"Yes."

"Do you know anyone who knows meditative music?"

"In the Caribbean, we get music from the sea."

"I could play the recorder!" I said.

Mom chuckled. "That would drive me crazy."

"What about Antoine?" I asked.

"Antoine?" Mom said. "Dad's driver?"

"Yeah," I said. "He's a jazz musician."

"That's right. He is," Mom said, nodding. "That's another good one, Ellie. We *will* get through this, won't we?"

Mom made me feel so good. I couldn't believe it. She was the one who was sick, and she was making *me* feel better.

I went to Alexa's house and didn't think about my mom's news all day. Later that night, I crawled into bed and it hit me again. I felt sick knowing that my mom was sick. A real-life nightmare had begun. Things were not good and would only get worse.

It Begins

The next day was cloudy, and all of Paris somehow looked sad too.

Our new, scary life had started. When I woke up, Mom and Dad had already gone to the doctor's office, and Munda walked me to the Metro station in the rain.

Sitting there alone on the train with my backpack in my lap, I wondered if my mother would ever go anywhere with me again. That week she went to the dentist, to a wig specialist, and finally to the hospital for treatment.

For the next few weeks, Mom would come and go. After each dose of chemotherapy, her skin seemed different, and she wore more makeup to cover the circles under her eyes. I knew Mom worried about how she might look to me, and I always thought she looked beautiful. But like she said, I'm biased.

When Mom felt better, she would go for a run with Dad. Then another round of treatments would start again, and she would get weaker and weaker.

With me, Mom tried to make everything better. After school I would walk into her room, and she would ask if I had a story. But I couldn't think of anything. When I heard her crying through the walls of the apartment, the only way to make the sound go away was to cry along with her.

Mom didn't seem to be getting any better. In fact, she was worse. One day, I came in from school, and she was sitting up in her bed.

She said, "I've got good news!"

Which of course surprised me.

"Dr. Manon has gotten me into a new test," she said. "It's a brand-new experiment that actually might work."

At first I was happy to hear this news. "That's great," I remember saying. Then I noticed the corner of Mom's lips turned downward, and I knew it was one of those things doctors do when there's nothing else to do.

"We don't know if it'll work," Mom said.

I knew the unsaid part of this sentence. *But we know what will happen if it doesn't.*

Mom had to go to a special hospital south of Paris and would stay there for three weeks straight. Before she left, she made plans for her return.

Munda was standing in the hallway upstairs in her white uniform, and on her head she had wrapped a blue-and-tan scarf, which sort of looked like waves at the beach.

"We get it worked out for you," she said. "The men, they are coming tomorrow, and they are bringing you your new bed in the morning and they're going to move you into the room where the office is now."

"Munda," Mom said. "I want those men to move my whole dresser, that one right there, move the whole thing downstairs to my new room." Then Mom looked at me. "And, Ellie, when I come back, let's you and I set up the mirrors and pictures just as they are now. Will you do that with me?"

"Yeah. Sure, Mom." I took a picture with my phone.

"Munda," Mom said. "If you and Calvert change everything in that room, I'll feel like I'm in a hospital. And I can't do that for very much longer."

"I am going to be a doctor one day," Munda said, "and I'll take care of everything."

"You'll make an excellent doctor," Mom said.

"And when you come back from the treatment," Munda said, "I'll show you how to tie a proper headwrap."

"I would like that," Mom said with a big smile.

While Mom was away at the specialized hospital, we made some changes in the apartment. A lot. Mom was going to move into the office on the main floor, and Dad's office was going to be in the living room.

A few men from Dad's work came over to the apartment and turned the living room into a business office. They pushed the couches and tables and lamps against the wall, and in their place they put desks and filing cabinets. A team of techies hooked up stacks of Henry's homemade supercomputers.

The movers carried Mom's dresser from my parents' upstairs room to Mom's new bedroom. Two guys from another company came and set up a bed that Dad had rented. It had the tilt buttons so Mom could sit up in bed. The maintenance man from Dad's office hung a television from the ceiling in Mom's new room.

Everything was ready, and I was so happy that Mom was finally coming back home and the treatment would *finally* be over. But when I saw her coming into the apartment in a wheelchair, I began to worry. A lot.

A New Life

Mom looked sick.

It wasn't just that she was sitting in a wheelchair. On her head she wore something like a swimmer's cap. Her eyebrows were thin, and under her eyes she had huge dark circles. That was a scary thing to see. But typical for my mom, she faked a smile and cracked a joke.

Her voice was faint and scratchy like she had a sore throat. "You think I look like I was in a fight?" she said. Her lips were dry and white. "Well, you should see the other guy!" She chuckled weakly. And then coughed.

Munda and the man from the hospital quickly took Mom into her new room in our apartment.

Dad and Henry were now working from the living room. Henry was British and spoke perfect French and Arabic. He always wore beautiful suits. This afternoon he was talking on the phone on the balcony. Dad took off his coat and tapped on the French doors, signaling Henry to come inside.

"Munda," Dad said when she came back into the living room, "are you sure you can handle this extra workload?"

"All in a day's work," she said.

"I just don't want you to get in over your head," Dad said as he sat at his desk.

"If it gets too rough," Munda said, "I will let you know. Now, don't you worry your pretty little head about a thing. I know the hard times from the Caribbean. Caring for the sick is part of life. You make sure we have money, and I'll take care of the rest."

"And that's that," Dad said. "I'll call the office and have the guys move you, too. Thank you."

Munda wrapped an arm around me and pulled me close, and for a moment, I felt like everything was going to be okay.

Henry came into the living room, and as he closed the French doors, the wind blew and messed up his hair.

He spoke with a clear British accent. "That's one for the record books."

"What's that?" Dad said, setting his phone down.

"Never actually spoken with the king of France before," Henry said, pronouncing it "Frahnce." "Poor old chap's got more money than the queen of England, but no throne!" He chuckled. "I couldn't bear reminding him of the fate of the last king of France. If the French people don't want you to be king, they have their ways of keeping you from the throne. Of course, I didn't mention that. I told him I'd be glad to manage his properties in North Africa."

"Good. He's got plenty of dough," Dad said. "He also wants to buy that olive plantation in Tunisia."

"Consider it done."

Henry checked a stack of blinking computers. He typed on a keyboard for a second.

"Righto," Henry said. "We are safe and secure in the new office. The algorithms are set now so that if you try to break in with four consecutive incorrect passwords, data destruction will begin."

"Hi Henry," I said.

"Hello, mademoiselle," he said, using the French term for "miss."

Dad said, "You know, Henry, that Munda is now Etta's new nurse."

"Yes, I did," Henry said. "I also know she's the reason for that delightful smell coming from the kitchen!"

"Indeed I am," Munda said. "Mr. Kerr, I will be getting to my work now."

"Don't let us get in your way," Dad said. He turned to Henry and said, "Get Munda's address and call Antoine and have him and the guys from the office move her belongings here."

"Righto," Henry said as he pulled out his mobile phone.

"Ellie," Dad said. "I need you to do three things."

I walked up to his desk. "What's that?"

"First, you have to do your homework on your own. Second, I need you to answer the home phone whenever you can. And third, spend as much time with Mom as possible. It will help her get better."

"She is going to get better," I said. "Isn't she?"

"Yes, she is."

Munda

The next day, the same men who had rearranged the furniture in the apartment came and moved Munda into the guest quarters next to Mom's new room. Munda was one of the smartest people I'd ever met. She seemed to know more about the soul and healing than she did history or math. She might have been from the Caribbean, but her accent made her sound like she came from the spirit world.

"I got strange habits," she said. "I believe in anything that can do some good. I do not want any lip from you about what it is that I believe in. I believe in God and Gaia alike. I pray to all the holy types. I take whatever works. Christianity, Islam, Judaism, animism, Hinduism, Buddhism, and any other 'ism' that can ease our burdens while our spirits are in this human experience. If we are all God's children, then we are *all* God's children. You hear me now, child?"

I nodded, and she opened the door.

Her room was alive with color. In a way it was my dream bedroom. She had a heart-shaped rug and a flowery bedspread. Across the far wall there was a string of colorful Tibetan prayer flags. Opposite the door a humongous strand of garlic hung from the ceiling to the floor. I pointed at it.

"That wards off evil," she explained.

On the wall next to a Star of David, she had a collection of crosses. There were Christian crucifixes with Jesus, plus-shaped Greek crosses, a fancy Celtic cross, and three Egyptian ankhs. Tiny models of the Parthenon, the Hagia Sophia, and a Mayan pyramid lined the baseboards. On the bedside tables sat a group of Buddhas and voodoo dolls of people and animals, and of creatures that looked like they had come from Shakespeare's plays.

"We are all God's children," Munda said. "All of us. You hear me now?"

I nodded.

"And every god that ever was or is or will be," Munda said, "is going to help us fight this battle. Now go on and get. I have got me some incense to burn. Someone has to keep away the evil spirits around here."

Picture Frame Collection

I thought Munda's voodoo might actually work. Either that or it might be the only thing that could save Mom.

Dad tried to explain to me what the experimental treatment was, but it was too confusing. Or maybe I didn't want to understand. He said something about the doctors trying new things. Which to me only meant they didn't know what they were doing. And if the doctors didn't know, then no one knew. We were just hoping for a miracle, a Munda Miracle.

As Mom spent more and more time in bed, our lives got busier and busier. People stopped by the apartment and brought flowers and food. Some brought hats and scarves. Munda organized everything. Dad even had her pack a few boxes for our move back to the States. I was supposed to help Mom with her picture-and-mirror collection, but since she napped so much, I decided to set it up on my own.

Mom's room was part hospital, part greenhouse. Machines and monitors next to her bed beeped and flashed while plants and flowers bloomed and grew on the opposite wall. In the corner, a dozen hats decorated a coat rack.

As Mom slept, slowly and quietly I organized the mirrors and pictures on the dresser. The frames were all different, some hammered copper and others tiny silver squares. They had come from a million places—Thailand and Mexico, Rabat and Washington. The photographs were also from all over the world.

There were shots of the Eiffel Tower, Tiananmen Square, and the Sydney Opera House. Some of the pictures Mom had taken for her Explore the World series that she had written. As I set them back up, it was like watching a movie of our life. There was a snapshot of Mom as a baby in an old metal windup swing. Her first birthday in front of a cake and a faded photo of a boy giving her a kiss on the cheek. There was one of me when I was three years old at the beach and one of Dad at his high school graduation. He was so young-looking. A couple of photographs were of Mom and Dad at parties or running, in the mountains or in the desert. The last frame I set up was a picture of Dad and me, fly fishing on a river in Montana.

Things could change so quickly.

It was just then that I heard a beeping sound coming from one of the medical machines. Mom buzzed her bed straight up, looked right at me, and started hacking. Her face turned bright red. Munda barreled into the room and hit some buttons and put a breathing mask over Mom's face.

I grabbed my backpack, ran upstairs, dove into my bed, and cried.

Mandy

Weeks went by, and nothing got better. When I came home from school, the first thing I'd do was check on Mom to see if she was awake. Most of the time she was asleep.

The phone rang like crazy, and I took messages for my dad's business and from my mother's well-wishers.

My aunt and uncle from Texas called once a week. They worried a lot. They were afraid of France because they said there were too many terrorists. When they asked about Mom's cancer, they wondered if the doctors were any good in France. I told them she had the best doctor in the world. But they didn't believe me.

People from the American School brought plants and flowers, and the whole house smelled like a garden. Ji Yoon and Bella and Alexa came by on the weekends, and we'd go to the café next to the flower shop and drink hot chocolate and do our homework together. It made me feel normal. They were my friends, and they helped me forget about the bad in my life.

One afternoon I went to check on Mom. The door

creaked when I opened it. Mom was sitting up in bed with her eyes closed, and she was wearing a turquoise-blue swimmer's cap.

She mumbled something.

"What's that, Mom?" I said. I was so excited to talk to her. I walked straight up to her bed.

"Where's Mandy?" she asked, cracking one eye open.

"Who?" I asked.

Munda had told me that people on pain medication can become confused and say things they don't mean and see things they don't see. And when that happens you just calm them down by agreeing with them.

"Yes, Mom," I said. "Yes. Munda is getting dinner ready."

"No," she said. There was a tiny grin on her lips, so I knew something was up. "I know what I'm saying," she said. "My medicine's worn off. I'm talking about Mandy the Mannequin."

"Mandy the Mannequin?" I said cautiously.

"The wig!" Mom said.

"Oh!" I said sarcastically. "You named your wig?"

"Yes."

"You are so weird, Mom," I said. "But you should wear the wig. That blue thing is awful."

"Have you not seen it on me?" she said.

"No."

"Get it out of the closet, and I'll try it on for you. Then we'll have a good laugh."

 50

It was great to see Mom feeling well. I opened the closet door, and there on the top shelf was a mannequin head wearing a wig.

"Beautiful, isn't she?" Mom asked sarcastically.

Mom peeled off the swim cap. Her head was completely bald, and I froze staring at it, at her. She was still very pretty to me.

Mom fixed the wig on her head. It was horrendous—like an electrified mop. Mom stuck out her tongue, and we broke out laughing.

"It's supposed to look nice," she said, taking the wig off. "But you have to wash the hair, comb it, and dry it first. I hardly have the strength to take a shower myself, much less bathe Mandy the Mannequin."

"Dad's right," I said. "You are strange."

"People are strange," she said.

"Like the song you like," I said.

"Yes," she said. "Jim Morrison."

Mom handed me the mannequin. "Put Mandy and her wig here on the bedside table," she said. "She can keep me company when no one's around."

I said, "We could watch TV!"

"No," she said. "Just sit."

I slipped the wig on the mannequin and set her next to a vase of fresh flowers. I scooted a chair up to her bed.

"Mom?" I said. "Why did you get cancer?"

"I wish I had an answer for you."

"How did you not know you had it for so long?"

She sighed. "This cancer I have is called the whispering disease because it comes and you just don't know it's there." Mom grabbed my hand and closed her eyes. The skin on her hands was wrinkly. We sat there saying nothing for a long time. Her breathing was heavy like it used to be after running.

Munda stomped down the stairs. "Ellie!" she called out. "Time for you to get in here and eat your dinner. Your mama needs her rest now. She has got a big doctor day tomorrow."

Munda walked into the room wearing a beautiful headwrap.

"What in the coconut happened to that wig?" she said, pointing at the mannequin.

"That's Mandy!" I said.

"It's looking discombobulated to me," Munda said. Then she laughed. "Maybe Munda will have to tie a headwrap on Mandy, too!"

Hurry, Hurry, Hurry

School days were always hectic with everyone running around, getting breakfast, and getting out the door. When you add a cancer patient to the mix, things get crazy.

Early the next morning Dad and Henry were already at work in the living room when I woke up. They were both on their phones, switching languages so fast from French to Arabic to English to Spanish that it sounded like a dozen people at a party.

Jean-Claude, the baker from downstairs, delivered a box of freshly baked bread, and the whole apartment smelled of warm butter. I stood between the living room, which was Dad's new office, and the old office, which was now Mom's bedroom. I snatched a croissant and ate it and watched and listened to both rooms.

In the living room, Henry answered his cell phone and laughed at something, then stepped out onto the balcony. Dad sat at the corner table talking on a cell phone and our regular house phone at the same time. The screens on his computers flashed green and red with the prices of companies from all over the world.

In Mom's room, Munda was getting Mom dressed for her doctor's appointment. With Mom sitting up in the tilted bed, Munda leaned over and began laying strips of fabric on Mom's bald head. Crimson red and olive green. Munda was the Picasso of headwraps.

"The colors," Munda said, "tell the universe who you are at that moment in time. Miss Etta, you got the color red for the fight in you, and green for the youth still in you."

Dad tapped on the French doors with his knuckle and waved Henry in.

Henry cracked open the doors. "Yes?" he said. "What's the matter?"

"Get back on the phone with Abdullah and tell him that the 'king' now wants to talk about selling the olive plantation in Tunisia."

"Righto," Henry said as he headed back to the balcony, scrolling through his phone. "This is fantastic. I absolutely love going to the Sahara."

"Henry," Dad said again. "Make sure you calmly say 'exploring a sale' and not 'we want to sell.' Those guys have more dough than sand, and they will tear you up if they think you are anxious. Play it cool and let them beat around the bush. That's their style."

In Mom's room, I heard Munda shriek. "You sit back down on this bed and let me finish my work," she said. "Lest I put that Mandy the Mannequin on your head."

They both started giggling.

"A real headwrap is like a good meal," Munda said. "It takes time."

The fabric was now tight around Mom's ears, but loose strips fell from the top of her head so that it kind of looked like locks of hair.

Munda would make an excellent doctor because she knew how to make people laugh.

"Etta Kerr, stop that moving around now," said Munda. "Am I going to have to put you in time out?"

Ever since she had moved into our apartment and started taking care of Mom, Munda had stopped being formal with Mom and Dad. They weren't Mr. and Mrs. Kerr anymore. Mom was now Etta, and Dad was Calvert. And Munda was in charge of the house. And that was that!

That afternoon I came in from school, and the whole apartment smelled of curry. I dropped my backpack on the floor and went into the kitchen to get a snack. While I ate one of the leftover croissants that Jean-Claude had delivered that morning, I peeked into the big pot that was on the stove. Curried chicken.

Dad was on his computers in the living room, and Henry was on the couch with Mom's laptop.

"Ah," Henry moaned. "That smell is driving me mad. I absolutely adore curry."

"You Englishmen," Dad said with a grin, "are fools for Indian food, aren't you?"

"I get the best curries from a man up in Montmartre," Munda said, coming out of Mom's room. "You want me to set you at the table tonight, deary?"

Dad nodded. "Good idea."

"Yes!" Henry said. "That would be wonderful."

Henry closed Mom's laptop and handed it to me. "Make sure you use the correct password. Otherwise, it will start to erase itself."

I nodded and then asked, "Did you read the stories?"

"Your mum suggested them to me," he said. "And after I updated the software on her computer last night, I gave it a go and read the Paris story until two in the morning."

"So you did like them?" I cheered.

"Of course!" he said. "Can't wait to see them in print."

"Me too," I said. "They're the best."

He grinned.

I took the laptop from Henry and hugged it. More than ever, I was determined to help Mom get her books published before she got too sick. As I stood there thinking of people we could ask to help, I heard the strangest sound coming from Mom's room.

Someone was playing a cello.

Keep on the Sunny Side

The music made me feel like everything was going to be all right.

I peeked through the half-open door to Mom's room and saw Antoine standing there with his cello. He was a thin man with black hair who worked at my dad's office as one of the drivers. At night he was a jazz musician. He was the nicest guy and he always gave me candy. He also insisted that we speak English with him so he could practice. Mom was sitting up in her bed while Antoine plucked on his cello. I went in to join them, and Antoine tossed me a piece of candy and kept playing.

Mom seemed to be feeling well that day and sang along.

Keep on the sunny side, always on the sunny side
Keep on the sunny side of life

Mom kept singing and clapping as she smiled at me and waved for me to come closer to her.

It will help us every day, it will brighten all the way
If we keep on the sunny side of life

"Hey, sweetie," she said as I leaned over and gave her a big hug and kiss.

I handed Mom her laptop, and she set it on the bed next to her. Antoine stopped playing the cello and leaned down to give me a kiss on the cheek.

"You want another good-good?" he said in his thick French accent.

"Yes," I said. "But in English, a *bonbon* is just called candy and not a good-good."

"You can say bonbon in English," Mom said. "That's perfectly fine too."

"We will call it a candy, like the princess wants," Antoine said as he pulled a box of chocolates from his cello case. "Etta? You want?"

"No thank you, Antoine," she said. "I don't want to upset my stomach any more than it already is."

Antoine handed me a fresh chocolate from the Neuhaus chocolate shop, which was just around the corner from our apartment.

"Ellie?" Mom said. "You got any jokes for me?"

I should have had a joke ready. Mom would have laughed at anything. I think a part of her was convinced that she could laugh her cancer away.

"Nothing funny, Mom," I said with a sigh.

"Ah!" Antoine said, pointing his finger up in the air like he had an idea. "I quote Voltaire, who says that life is a funny play in which everyone forgets to laugh. Ha-ha!"

Mom chuckled. "Good one! I'm sticking with

Voltaire," she said. She pushed the button that raised the top part of her bed so that she could sit up even more. "I've got a joke for you—a new one from the treatment center."

I sat in the chair next to her bed, knowing the joke was going to be corny.

"How can nurses handle all the work they have in busy hospitals?"

"I don't know, Mom."

"Because they have a lot of patients!"

"Oh, Mom!" I said, bowing my head in embarrassment. "That's terrible."

"Ah!" Antoine said as he finally got the joke. "That is superb, Etta. *Patients* is a double entendre, a double hearing. You hear it two times; it has two meanings. It's a pun. Yes, yes. Very . . . punny! Ha-ha!"

"Another good one, Antoine," Mom said. "Ellie, you don't have to be ashamed of my bad jokes. It's only Antoine here. And besides, I don't care. I try to laugh as much as I cry. Both make me feel better. And with you, I'd rather laugh."

While Antoine kept playing his cello, Mom reached over to touch my hand.

"Ellie," she said in a serious voice. "Cancer may take my *life*, but it is not going to take my *laugh*. Okay? That does not mean that life or cancer is a joke. Antoine's music and laughing help me get through the hard parts. Some women in my treatment center tell hilarious jokes, and it makes us laugh, and that helps the medicine go down."

"It doesn't surprise me," I said.

"What?"

"That you'd be laughing at cancer."

"Why?"

"Because you're the happiest person in the world."

Mom closed her eyes and grinned.

"Hearing you say that," she said, "makes me happy."

Antoine started playing "Keep on the Sunny Side" on the cello again.

The other part of that sunny-side song says that there's a dark and troubled side of life too. I could feel the clouds rolling in, getting darker and darker.

Rainstorm

The sunny side of our lives got turned upside down.

Clouds surrounded Paris as storms marched in. I tried to time the space between the lightning and the thunder, but could never tell how far away anything was or where it was coming from. It seemed the beginning was the end, and the end was the beginning.

Words like *surgery*, *chemotherapy*, and *radiation* rained down on every conversation.

Nothing made sense.

For days after treatment, Mom couldn't sleep at night. In the daytime she was extra grouchy. She had a plastic thing called a port hanging out of her left arm because they were giving her so many shots. She said it hurt. She complained about being constipated, which used to be something to joke about, but it wasn't anymore. She even breathed funny now. Not ha-ha funny. Like strange, scary kind of breathing. The kind of wheezing that really makes you afraid that your Mom is going to . . .

Enter Munda.

Munda would not stand for anything negative. She convinced us that a positive outlook could heal my mother. Munda also had her own treatments for Mom.

Every hour Munda gave Mom a bright green smoothie. Dad followed the doctor's orders and gave Mom her pills and shots. On the bedside table, next to Mandy the electric-hair mannequin, there were at least six bottles of different pills for different things.

Some days Mom was sicker than normal. On those days the storms swirling around the Eiffel Tower seemed to crash through the windows and into our apartment, pelting us with the saddest rain ever.

Munda made a schedule for spending time with Mom. We would trade off sitting with her throughout the day, and that's exactly what we'd do: sit in a chair next to her bed and wait. I wanted to help, but I didn't want to wait because I was afraid of what I was waiting for.

Munda sat with her during the day while I was at school and Dad and Henry worked in the living room. After school, I'd sit in her room with my homework. She slept most of the time. At dinnertime, I would leave, and Dad would stay with her during the night.

One day Mom was wide awake, sitting up in bed, just looking at me. She smiled. I guess to some, my mom's bald head and dark circles under her eyes were scary. I don't know how to describe it, but to me somehow my mom was as beautiful as she had always been.

"Hey, Mom?" I said, hoping we could talk like we used to. My mom was always a good listener. You could tell her anything and everything, and she would just sit there and listen.

Her voice was hoarse and faint. "Yes, Ellie."

"Do you want me to read one of your books to you?"

"They're manuscripts, sweetie," she said. "Books are published . . . except for mine of course!" She chuckled at her own joke.

"Can I?" I asked again.

"I don't have . . . ," she said in a weak voice. "I don't have the strength today."

"I'll do the reading," I said, more determined than ever. "You just sit back and relax."

"Okay."

Mom closed her eyes while I read the first chapter of the Explore the World series.

There's something exciting about reading a book—I mean a manuscript—before anyone else in the whole world. This is what literary agents and editors get to do. It's like having your private library filled with books that only you have read.

"Mom," I asked. "What are you going to do with your stories?"

"What's that?" she said, waking up.

"What are you going to do with these stories?" I said. "They are so good."

"What am I going to do with them?"

"Yeah, I think they're great. Really. I'm not just saying that."

"You're biased."

"What?"

"That means you're an unfair judge of my books."

"I am not biased," I said defensively. "I'm a good reader."

"It's not that," she said, panting. "It's just that editors don't trust the children of writers because the kids always say they like what their parents have written, mostly because they don't want their parents to go broke."

"Huh?"

"Ellie, I've done what I can with those stories. I wrote them. They just need more time. Something I don't have a lot of."

"Maybe we should ask Uncle Paul."

Her voice faded. "All things in due time, in due time."

She closed her eyes and fell asleep while I was sitting there. I put the manuscript away, and Dad came in and traded places with me.

Every evening he would sit by Mom's bed whether she was awake or not. He tried to show that he wasn't scared or sad, but I knew he was both by the way his smile never turned upward.

He would plop down next to her, not talk, just sit there all night long and hold her hand while she slept.

Some days I'd find him asleep in the armchair next to Mom's bed, his arm stretched out, and his hand still wrapped around her fingers.

Excuse Me

One day, a funny thing—or more like an embarrassing thing—happened.

I came in from school, threw my backpack on the floor, and grabbed one of Jean-Claude's croissants. The living room was a mess, and Henry and Dad had apparently left in a rush. On the table there was a note from Munda saying that she had gone shopping for dinner.

I spoke softly, not wanting to wake Mom. "Hello?"

Nothing.

I crept toward her room and peeked through the crack in the door. Mom's bed was empty. I immediately thought the worst.

Then I heard the loudest and longest burp I'd ever heard in my life.

"Mom?" I called out, hoping it was her and not someone who shouldn't be there.

I rounded the corner of her room and peered into the bathroom. Mom was sitting at the vanity. It seemed strange that she was out of bed by herself. The mirrors surrounding her reflected her image from all sides. I could see both of our faces looking back at us.

I said, "Was that what I think it was?"

"Ella Elizabeth Kerr," Mom said into the mirror. "I didn't know you were home yet. Why didn't you tell me you were here? And yes, it was what you think it was."

She chuckled. "The burps are making me feel strangely strong today."

Sometimes it's easier to talk to someone when you're speaking to a reflection. I moved closer, and the mirrors seemed to make endless copies of us. For that moment, everything that was wrong with our world vanished into infinity, a place where all the hurt faded away.

Then Mom did it again. She let out the second largest and longest burp I'd ever heard in my life.

She looked at me and broke into a giggle, and then she braced herself on my shoulders and we laughed.

Hectic

Sometimes Mom had to go to the doctor earlier than usual and our mornings became extra crazy.

The routine was thrown off schedule by several things. First, Munda had to get Mom ready, which took a lot of time to tie her headwrap on and do her makeup. One of Dad's clients telephoned from New Zealand, and since they were ahead of us in time, he had to take the call at seven in the morning. Henry came in at seven thirty instead of eight, and he started working on his computers.

Like always, Jean-Claude came with bread for the day, but since Munda was working with Mom, Jean-Claude decided to stay and help out too. He got on his phone and called the woman at the outdoor market to bring up some fresh fruits and vegetables.

Then Antoine came in with his cello.

I ran upstairs, got dressed, ran downstairs, and ate a croissant. I knew I was going to be late for school. I went into Mom's room, where Munda was still fixing Mom's makeup. She had already spent a half hour tying on the headwrap, which on that day was a golden taffeta-like fabric. Munda had twisted it to look like blond locks. I watched Munda sketch eyebrows on my mother's face. Next, she covered up the dark circles under Mom's eyes. The final two touches: a thick layer of red lipstick and two diamond earrings.

Presto chango. Mom was dressed up!

I could hear Dad in the living room, hanging up the phone. Then he said *bonjour* to the fruit woman, who had just walked in with a basket of food.

Henry muttered something about his computers.

Dad shook his head and stormed into Mom's room. "Can you believe how nuts this is? What in the heck is Antoine doing here with his cello? I thought he was giving you a ride to the doctor!"

Then Dad looked at Mom, and his jaw dropped. Seeing her up close must have changed everything for him. "Wow!" he said, his voice softened. "You look so beautiful!"

"Thank you," Mom said as she pointed to Munda, who was standing beside the bed. "Thank Munda," she said. "She's the artist here."

"I don't know what we'd do without you, Munda," Dad said. "I really don't."

"Calvert?" Mom cut in. "What's going on out there?"

"We're just having troubles with the sale of the olive plantation," he explained. "The deal has to be finished while we're still here, or it'll cost us buckets of dough."

Mom interjected. "We don't want that," she said. "I

would feel guilty if my sickness cost us more money than it already has."

"Don't worry," said Dad. "I just got off the phone with Helen in New Zealand, and she's flying here tomorrow for a meeting. Besides, you have your own things to worry about."

I could tell Dad's head was in a million places.

"What is the fruit woman doing here?" he said. "She brought apples and bananas and carrots. Looks like she might move in and cook for us!"

"Jean-Claude called her," I explained, "because Munda is going to be gone all day and we won't have anything for dinner and you and Henry won't have any lunch."

"Oh," he said. "That was nice."

"Maybe she's . . . ," Mom said, "maybe she's playing 'I'm going on a picnic' with those apples and bananas and carrots."

I was the only one who laughed at Mom's joke. It wasn't that good, but it was amazing that she found funny things everywhere. Munda was picking up Mom's clothes at that point, and Dad must have been thinking about work.

Antoine started playing his cello loudly, and it seemed to calm the whole apartment. *Blum, blum, blum.* Dad poked his head out of Mom's room.

"Antoine?" Dad called to him. "What are you doing here?"

"Madame Kerr asked me to come and play some

cello for her today before we go to the *docteur*."

"You're supposed to be taking her to treatment," Dad said, still aggravated. He turned back into Mom's room. "Etta? Did you ask Antoine—"

"I did."

With a handful of clothes in her arms, Munda pulled me to the side.

"Time to go to school. And time for your mother's cello lesson before she goes to the doctor."

"Cello lesson?" Dad said, scratching his head. "Have I missed something here?"

Mom sat on the edge of the bed. "It's not a lesson, Calvert. It's for my meditation. It's relaxing. You need to read something other than business journals. There are so many alternative treatments for cancer, and meditation helps."

It always bothered me when Mom and Dad were tense.

"I gotta go, Mom," I said, butting in. I gave her a light hug because of her makeup.

Dad gave me a kiss on the forehead. "I'll see you when you get home, okay. Don't worry. Everything's going to be fine."

Munda went to her room, and I stepped into the hallway. I waited between the two rooms and listened to the whole house. Out in the living room, Jean-Claude, the fruit woman, and Henry listened to Antoine play the cello. From Mom's room, I heard my parents' conversation.

"It's inevitable, Calvert," Mom said.

"That's true for everyone," he said.

"Calvert! Be realistic," she said. "I have terminal cancer."

"If you're going to live, it's not terminal."

"You're right," Mom said, calming down. "But at the same time, I can't be in denial. I know how bad it is, Calvert. I can feel it. It's . . . it just doesn't feel right."

I peeked through the crack in the door.

"Are you sure you want to stay here in Paris?" he said in a calm voice. "You really don't want to go back to the States?"

"I'm not going," she said, sitting up on the bed. "Let's be frank about this."

Dad tried to lighten it up. "The name's Calvert, not Frank!"

Mom cracked a smile. "Calvert, I love you but I don't want to go back to the States," she said. "I think it's foolish for me to go anywhere. First off, I don't think traveling on an airplane for eleven hours would do me any good. And then we would move into a new house in a new city, and you and Ellie wouldn't be able to start your lives because you'd be caring for me without Munda around. And frankly, we'd be waiting for the inevitable."

"But . . ." Dad tried to cut in.

"It's true."

"What about . . ." Dad tried again.

"We know how bad this is," Mom said, cutting him

off. "I am as comfortable here as I will be anywhere. I love Paris. It is without question my favorite city in the world. And we have so many wonderful people here.

"The three of us—this is our family," she continued. "Dr. Manon and her team are considered the best in the world. Ellie's in a good school. We have Munda and we have all these expats and even the shopkeepers are helping out. Antoine's cello is wonderful for me. And you still make me laugh! Yes, there are good things about going to the US. If my parents were still alive, I might say let's go and get my mother and father to help out. If I'd had any contact with my sister in the last fifteen years, then I might call her, but I don't know her anymore. My brother Paul is busy with his books and our old friends back home are busy with their lives, and you know it's not my style to call and beg for help. Let's just stay here and enjoy the time we have. Besides, I love France. I love the lifestyle. I like the pace of life here. I even like it that stores still close on Sundays. I love everything about being here."

As soon as Mom finished talking, Dad bowed his head for a second.

"You're right," he said. "And, it's your decision."

Martians

Mom's next tests were called a CAT scan and a PET scan. I didn't know what CAT or PET stood for, but it had nothing to do with a pet or a cat, unfortunately. Dad told me it was basically a fancy X-ray machine.

A few days later Dr. Manon planned to visit us at home. I might have only been eleven and 294/365^{ths} at the time, but I knew a doctor coming to your house was a bad sign. They don't stop by to tell you everything is okay.

I had to leave. So I went to my friend Alexa's apartment, which was just on the other side of the park in front of the Eiffel Tower. Alexa's family was from South Africa. Her father was a tall Zulu, and her mother was a blond Afrikaner. Afrikaners are the descendants of Dutch settlers of South Africa, and they speak English with an accent. Alexa was a perfect mix of her parents. Always tan and a face so pretty that she would never need makeup. Their apartment was a mix too. Fancy Dutch paintings and tribal spears and shields decorated the place.

Alexa's mother was going to the beauty salon, and she invited us to come along and get our hair cut as well. Alexa and I decided to get the same exact haircut. Shoulder length, curled around to the face. The two women cutting our hair were about twenty, and they both had spiky pink hair and tons of earrings and face rings.

"Would you like to dye your hair today?" one of them asked with a British accent.

"Don't worry," the other said. "It's temporary."

Alexa and I looked at each other and burst out laughing.

"Should we ask my mom?" Alexa wondered.

I needed something different in my life. "It's temporary? Really?" I asked the stylist.

"It'll wash right out in a few showers."

"I'm in," I said.

"Me too," Alexa said.

We both chose our favorite color—lime green.

On the walk back to Alexa's place, we cut across the park in front of the Eiffel Tower.

"Hey!" Alexa said with a mischievous grin. "Champs de Mars means the Field of Mars, right . . . and we have green hair!"

"We are Martians!" I said.

"Mama! Kan ons gaan speel?" Alexa asked her mother in Afrikaans if we could go play.

"Yes," she said back in English. "Just don't go far. Ellie will have to be home soon. Munda is going to make you wash your hair tonight, you know."

"Oh no!" I said as Alexa pulled me away.

The Field of Mars is a long and grassy park.

That afternoon it was filled with people walking with baby carriages and old men and women sitting on benches. There were a few runners, which of course made me think of my parents.

Alexa's mother sat down and knitted while we took off with our green hair, pretending we were on Mars. Alexa pointed toward some pedal carts and we ran back and forth, making weird noises and faces at anyone who would pay any attention to us.

We passed a little boy blowing soap bubbles, and we made the ghost sound, *whoo*, and he started to cry. As he ran off screaming to his mother, Alexa and I cut through the shadow of the Eiffel Tower.

It was exactly what I needed to do. I was so worried about Mom that I had become stressed out. I needed to go crazy. Alexa eyed a group of American boys in khakis, white tennis shoes, and baseball caps.

We sneaked up behind them.

"You—are from—America," I stammered in my Martian voice.

"We are from Mars," Alexa said like an alien, twisting her hands in the air.

A boy in a baseball cap stopped and turned around to face us.

He gritted his teeth. "Yes, we are Americans." He raised his arms. "We eat Martians in America! Ahhh!"

PAUL AERTKER

Then he chased us across the grass, where we ended up back at Alexa's mother's bench.

Home base.

But unfortunately, it was time to go back to our real homes and our real lives.

Storm

Storm clouds rolled across the sky as I ran home, and the feeling of being totally free faded.

Dr. Manon was pacing in Mom's room when I came in. The door was cracked open, and I watched and listened. I was just in time to hear what I didn't want to hear.

The doctor's white lab coat blocked most of my view. Dr. Manon was super friendly, and she had wavy hair and spoke in a soft voice. She spoke both French and English perfectly.

"Etta," I heard Dr. Manon say to Mom. "The cancer on the left side is, in fact, shrinking."

That was good news, but the way she spoke told me there was a *but* coming.

"But," Dr. Manon said, "the other side of your abdomen has been compromised and—"

"Psst," I heard Munda hissing from the kitchen. She whispered, "Ella Elizabeth. That is a private meeting. Your mother and father will discuss it with you when they choose. Now get away from that door. Oh my! What in the coconut have you done to your hair?"

She patted my head.

"It washes out," I said, sitting at the table.

Munda put dinner on the table and sat down with me. It was fish with curried garlic and couscous. A while later Dad and Dr. Manon came out of Mom's room.

"Oo la!" Dr. Manon said to me. She gently touched my head. "Look at this hair!"

"What did you do, Ellie?" Dad said.

"Alexa and I got our hair dyed."

"I can see that," Dad said.

"We got our hair cut from the British girls with pink hair, and they wanted to dye ours."

Dr. Manon said, "I think it looks beautiful."

"It washes out," I said.

"Keep it for as long as you can," Dr. Manon said. She turned to Dad and said that she would call in the morning. Then she left.

Munda told me to say good night to Mom. When I went into her room, Mom was in bed and her eyes were closed. I could tell she had been crying. Her eyes were bright red like she had been stung by bees.

She opened her arms for a hug. "Pretty green hair," she said. "Perfect for a girl turning twelve."

I could feel an ugliness storming through my body. "I want you to be at my birthday this summer. And, I'm eleven and nine-twelfths."

She reached out to touch me, and her cold palm rested on my arm. "You're such a wonderful child," she said softly, "a perfect person. You know that? You know that you didn't even kick in my womb. You danced."

She closed her eyes and moaned from either pain or a happy memory or maybe both. I couldn't tell. I was too upset that I couldn't do anything to help her.

"I remember the first time I felt you," she said, half-awake, half-asleep. "Your little arms shot up and hit me in the ribs! And those beautiful legs of yours pushed down and made me have to go to the bathroom all the time. Arms up, legs down—that was you. The disco queen!"

She smiled at me, and tears fell from her eyes.

Mom asked, "Did you have that fish for dinner?"

"Why are you asking about fish?" I snapped back.

Mom smiled. "Munda thinks she can cure cancer with garlic and fish."

I knew I had been snippy with her, but I didn't know what to do. I wiped her cheeks with a tissue and told her it would be okay.

"I know it's hard for you," she said, now squeezing my hand. "What I hope for is that this cancer goes into a very long remission. That is possible. I can't lie to you. A cure, for me at this stage, is doubtful. Let's just hope it stays away for a long, long time. And you stay with me. You are the light that keeps me going."

I didn't know what to say. I didn't want a sick mom. I wanted to be with my friends. There were so many feelings, all at the same time, stirring inside.

"Who's going to take care of me?" I yelled.

"Nothing's normal here. I wish we had never come here. I hate France! I wish we had just stayed in the US, where everything was fine. There wasn't any cancer in America when we were there. Why did we have to come here? For some stupid job? So you could get sick and . . . ?"

Munda and Dad shot into the room, and I ducked around them to cut out of the room. I stamped up each and every step and slammed the door to my room. At that moment I hated everything. Myself included.

Outside, there was thunder and lightning, and I cried.

The Outcome

The next day—or maybe it was a week or two later. I don't know.

Nothing seemed right. I came home from school, threw my backpack on the floor, and ate Nutella on a baguette for a snack. With the first bite, the chocolate started sticking in my throat. Even chocolate tasted wrong.

Munda was in her room praying, and Henry was at the computer in the corner working quietly. It was nighttime by the time Mom and Dad came back to the apartment. Dad was pushing Mom in the wheelchair. From the way he looked, the doctor's visit had not gone well.

Munda poked her head out.

Dad looked at her, took his glasses off, and rubbed his eyes.

"It's everywhere," he said.

I knew he meant the cancer was everywhere in Mom's body. I had overheard them talking once that this was the one thing they did not want to happen. If the cancer spreads, it will grow even faster somewhere else in her body.

I followed Mom and Dad into the hospital-at-home room. Munda helped Mom into bed.

"Open the curtains," Mom said. "It's at the top of the hour, isn't it?"

Dad glanced at his watch. "Nine fifty-seven."

I opened the curtains, and there on the right side stood the Eiffel Tower, shining in a bronze light. A few minutes later thousands of blinking strobe lights sparkled up and down the iron legs.

"The flashing lights make the tower look like a giant mirror," Mom said. "It's beautiful, isn't it?"

"It's awesome," I said.

Dad took off his jacket and set it on the chair next to Mom's bed. He placed his hands on the back of another chair.

"Mom's tired," he said. "So, I'll explain what's going on."

I slumped to the floor.

"Your Mom is strong," Dad said. "And that's exactly what we're going to have to rely on—her strength—from here on out. Dr. Manon has given us two choices. Neither option is good. One is to increase the chemo-therapy and use radiation. It might make your Mom live longer, but she would have to stay in a special-care center, and the outcome unfortunately still wouldn't change."

The outcome, I thought.

"Mom has already made the decision," Dad said. "It is hers to make. She is going to stay here with us in this house, look at the Eiffel Tower, and be with me and you and Munda."

"Isn't that better?" I said hopefully.

"Yes," Mom said softly. Her dry lips cracked when she spoke. "To see you . . . yes that's better. I sound like the wolf in 'Little Red Riding Hood.'"

She was still trying to be positive.

"It is better," Dad said in a serious tone. "It's a question of living in the chemotherapy center or living here at home."

"So what about the cancer?"

"This is where we count on our spirit," Munda said as she fixed Mom's pillow.

Munda sounded like she was talking to us from heaven. Goose bumps covered my whole body.

Munda helped me up from the floor and put her arm around me.

"Deary," she said, "the good Lord is going to do what he is going to do, and you got to do what you need to do. And the only tool you got now is love. We are going to wash your Mama in love. She is alive right now. She is beautiful, and we celebrate it."

For the next month or so, everything was quiet. Mom slept a lot. The machines around her bed seemed to be more alive than she was. Beeping and beeping. Her skin looked yellow; her lips sprouted tiny sores.

Munda, Dad, and I took turns sitting by her side, wiping her forehead with damp towels. Antoine came and played the cello. Mom slept. Jean-Claude brought something to eat every day. Munda cooked garlic and curry for breakfast, lunch, and dinner, hoping to ward off evil spirits. Henry, dressed in his usual suit and tie, worked quietly by himself in the living room. Parents from the school stopped by. The head of school even wrote me a personal letter. My whole class signed a huge get-well card for my mother, which I pinned to the wall in Mom's room. Ji Yoon, Alexa, and Bella came by a few times, and we would hang out in my room. But there was always a cloud hanging over my bed.

We waited. I didn't have to ask for what.

Then one day everything changed. One morning, after weeks of barely being able to breathe, Mom woke up with a big burst of energy.

All of a sudden everything seemed fine.

Except Munda. She became worried, very worried.

Feel Good

When I came downstairs, I could hear singing.

Singing? I thought. *Mom?*

She could barely talk the day before, and now she was singing.

"Whoa," she sang. "Whoa, whoa."

She kept singing, and I ran back upstairs. Dad was coming out of the bathroom.

"What's going on?" Dad said, putting on his glasses.

"It's Mom," I said. "She's awake!"

"Good," he said. "It's time for her medicine."

"No, Dad! It's different this time."

"What?"

"I mean she's acting like there's nothing wrong," I said. "Like maybe it's gone into redemption!"

"It's remission, sweetheart."

"Whatever," I said, practically bouncing up and down. "Who cares? Let's go. I think it's gone forever, maybe. Pleeeease."

I took off down the stairs. Dad followed. Munda came out of her room, holding a voodoo doll.

"Ellie!" Munda yelled at me. "Stop your singing. Your mama is trying to get some sleep."

"*She's* singing," I said.

"Etta?" Munda asked. She glanced at the voodoo doll as if she had done something to make the singing happen.

"Yes," I said, pumping my arms.

"I think the pain medicine might be making her go crazy," Dad said to Munda. "How much did you give her last night?"

"Singing?" Munda said again, ignoring Dad's question. She shook her head and stared at the doll.

"She is singing," Munda said, nodding her head. "Oh Lord. She is singing. Oh Lord. Oh Lord."

From just outside her room, we could hear Mom humming a song. Dad started to open Mom's door, but Munda moaned.

"Mmm," she said with her eyes closed. "This is not good."

"What?" my dad said, glaring at Munda. "What's wrong with singing?"

"Nothing," Munda said, as she turned to put the doll back in her room. "I will fix the breakfast. We have got a big day in front of us."

"What do you mean?" Dad said, still with his hand on the doorknob.

"I can feel it, and I know what's happening," Munda said, "and that's that."

As she went into the kitchen to fix breakfast, she hummed "Kumbaya, My Lord" to herself.

Dad opened the door, and Mom was standing next

to the bed! Wearing a silk robe and a sock hat, she smiled and waved her cane at us. She held the walking stick like a microphone and went back to her singing.

"Whoa!" she sang, making the weirdest faces, "whoa, whoa."

She pointed the cane at us when she sang, and then she smiled, took off her hat, and smoothed her bald head. It was the first time in a long time that she had color in her face.

Even though his voice was not the best, Dad didn't miss a beat. He sang along with her.

They pretended to play the saxophone, and they practically fell into each other, hugging. Then they opened their arms, and we had a group hug. It was the best.

Mom broke the hug and looked at us and said, "Let's go to the top of the Eiffel Tower today!"

"Look me in the eyes," Dad said to Mom. "How do you feel? Do you feel loopy today? A little too much medicine maybe?"

"Loopy?" she said. "No. That pain medicine makes me feel dizzy. I hate it. I haven't taken it in three days."

"What?" Dad asked, his voice rising.

"I just wanted to see if I could do without," Mom said. "Every time you or Munda gave me the medicine, I didn't swallow it. I've been spitting the pills out and putting them under Mandy's wig!"

I went over to the other side of the bed where Mandy the Mannequin was, and sure enough, there they were. Under Mandy's wig there were dozens of squished white pills. It was gross. But that was my mom! It was so weird seeing her excited. Like a kid. Singing and cracking jokes and not taking her medicine.

"So you want to go to the Eiffel Tower," Dad said, hesitantly. "What's that all about?"

"Calvert," she said. "I wrote a book about the Eiffel Tower. I like the place, you know. And right now I actually feel . . . okay."

"What about infections?" Dad shot back. "You could catch anything. I don't want you to get sick."

"I am sick already."

"I don't want you to get any sicker," Dad said. "An infection could be . . . could set you back."

Mom stared at him with a sassy look. "I want to go to the Eiffel Tower today. And, as Munda would say, that's that." And then Mom stuck out her tongue at him.

"I'll make some phone calls," Dad said, "and see if we can bypass the lines."

"Tell them I don't have time to wait in line," Mom said.

After breakfast Munda whispered to my father. "This is no remission, you know."

"I know what you're talking about Munda," Dad said. "I've read plenty. Maybe that's what it is—her body is shutting down, and this is just her extra energy trying to escape. And then again, maybe it's real remission. No one really ever knows. You may have your feelings, but I know that nobody knows for sure. All I know is that at least for today, my wife, Ellie's mom, is alive."

"You know as well as I," Munda whispered. "It is her spirit, coming to say good-bye to us."

"Maybe yes," Dad said. "Maybe no."

"Are we really going to go to the Eiffel Tower?" I said. "Can I invite a friend? Can I call Ji Yoon or Bella or maybe Alexa—she lives right on the other side of the park. Can I?"

"No, my deary," Munda said as she headed back into Mom's room. "Not today. Today, you go with your family. Just the three of you."

Email

The black-and-white headwrap was already wrapped around Mom's head, and Munda was busy working on her makeup.

Dad stuck his head into the room. "The interior minister is giving us VIP access to the tower," he said. "Antoine will be here in an hour to pick us up."

Munda finished getting Mom dressed, and then she left the room. Mom, using her cane, hobbled toward the bathroom.

"Mom?"

"Yeah?"

"Can I use your computer?"

"Do you know the password?"

"Same as your email," I said, turning on the laptop. "One-two-three-I-am-me. Right?"

"Right," she said, closing the door to the bathroom. "A password should make you feel good when you type it in. That way you always start out on the right foot."

I typed in the password. *123Iamme*. Colorful balloons rose up on the screen.

"If you see some balloons pop up," Mom said from

behind the closed door. "That was Henry's idea."

I had a message from Vicky. Ever since I had told her Mom's cancer was getting worse, Vicky had started writing and texting more often, and her messages had sad faces instead of happy faces.

Mom asked, "Did you hear back from Vicky?"

"I did," I said, still reading the message. "She said she might come and visit this summer. She said that her mom and dad and she are so sorry about your illness. Your friend together, forever, Vicky."

"That's sweet," Mom said. "It's splendid to think that you might actually be connected to some people forever."

I closed the app and saw that Mom had five Explore the World stories on the desktop.

Then the weirdest thing happened. Just as I was about to click on the Paris story, Mom's email account dinged and popped up and said that she had just received a message. I saw the title of her series, Explore the World, in the reference line, and I immediately knew it was from a publisher.

Yes, I thought.

She was going to get her books published. Someone wanted to publish her book!

"Hey, Mom!" I screamed across her room.

Mom opened the door to the bathroom. She was wearing a silk rose jacket that Ji Yoon's mom had given her.

"What is it?"

"Hey, Mom. You got a publisher—from London—for your book series! Somebody just sent you an email. . . ."

"Did you read it?"

"Well, no."

"At this point, it wouldn't be a publisher, but maybe an agent who would represent my work. I can promise you that with the way things are in America and in the world, now is not the right time for this book. It's probably another rejection letter."

"What if it's not?"

"Keep hoping."

"Can I open the email?"

"Sure, why not?"

I double-clicked the icon, but I was so nervous that I didn't do it right. I clicked again. Mom was now leaning toward the mirror, touching up her lipstick. I read the email to her.

> *Dear Sarah,*
> *Many thanks indeed for sending us EXPLORE THE WORLD for our consideration. Although we think you have some good ideas, unfortunately EXPLORE THE WORLD is not going to be one for us. We sincerely wish you all the best in finding a publisher in the future. Kind regards.*

I said, "Who's Sarah?"

"This is a rejection letter, Ellie, and the editor or

the agent just got my name wrong."

"Got the name wrong?"

"Editors and literary agents are busy."

"You're busy too," I said. I was so mad. "You're a mom and a writer. *And*, you're fighting cancer."

"To them, I am an 'un.'"

"An un?" I said, scrunching up my nose.

"Un means unpublished."

"Yeah, but . . ."

"Yeah, but," Mom finished. "You're right, Ellie. There's always a first time for everything."

"I still think it's rude that they sent you an email and called you Sarah when your name is Etta," I spat. "You should write them back and tell them . . . and tell them . . . I don't know, tell them something."

"You write them," Mom said.

"Really?"

"Really."

"What do I say?"

"Ask them who Sarah is," Mom said sarcastically.

I hit the reply button in the email, and it brought up a new screen. I was ready to give that publisher or editor or whatever she was a piece of my mind. Thanks to Ji Yoon, Bella, Alexa, and the American School of Paris, I knew bad words in four languages. I looked over at my mother in the bathroom, looking at herself in the mirror.

"Mom!" I growled.

"Be kind," she said. "Be quick and professional; it

will pay off in the end."

I typed *There seems to be a mistake. Who's Sarah? Sincerely, Etta.*

And I sent it.

It felt good, just to say you're wrong. Bleh. I was glad I could do something to stick my tongue out at all the publishers of the world who obviously didn't know that kids want to read books about kids who travel and save the world.

Mom was hunched over the sink, swaying. I could see her eyes in the mirror. They were wide open. Her face went totally white and then red as blood.

"Mom?" I screamed.

"Oh," she moaned, holding her back. "Give me that medicine . . . pain medicine . . . right there . . . on there on the . . . on the thingy." She dropped down to the floor on one knee, holding her hand in the sink. I threw the laptop on the bed and started looking on the bedside table for the medicine.

I was so nervous. "You mean the . . . ," I said, "the dexa . . . dexa . . . ?"

"Yeah," she panted. She was breathing like crazy.

"Mooom!" I screamed. I heard the phone drop in the kitchen.

"Hand . . . hand me," she panted. "Yeah, hand me the other one too . . . starts with a *d*."

"Daaad!" I screamed, just as he was coming into the room. "Mundaaa! Help!"

"What? What? Get the Dim . . . ," Dad said as he

stomped, looking around for the medicine. He nearly knocked Mandy off the bedside table. "Ah! What's the name of that stupid stuff?"

"I already gave it to her," I told him.

Mom threw the pills in her mouth. She leaned over the sink and tried to catch her breath.

"Sit down, Etta," Dad said, scooting the wheelchair up to her.

Mom sat and bowed her head. A few minutes later she looked up and spoke.

"This medicine," she spoke in a slow drawl, stretching the words out, "makes me so drowsy . . ." She grinned, letting us know that she was okay and that she was trying to make a joke. "So let's have coffee. Lots of it!"

"Etta?" Dad said. "I don't think this is a very good idea."

"I'll be all right," she said. "The first pill took care of the pain, and the second took care of the anxiety." She stood up. "I'll be fine. Do we have a driver?"

"Antoine will be here shortly," Dad said, as he stepped out of the room.

"So what did you type?" Mom said, now standing with her cane.

"What did I what?" I had no idea what she was talking about. "Type?"

"The email?" she said. "What did you write in the email?"

"Oh, I almost forgot," I said. "I wrote, 'There seems

to be a mistake. Who's Sarah? Sincerely, Etta.' Is that good?"

"Perfect," Mom said. "In due time, sweetie."

"Mom?" I asked. "How do you get published for the first time if you have to already be published in the first place? It doesn't make any sense."

"I don't have an answer for that," Mom said. "One of the problems with computers and word-processing software being everywhere is that everyone can type, more or less, but typing doesn't make a person a writer; it makes a person a typist. And in today's world, things are hurried for writers, agents, editors, and publishers, alike, so we all end up missing opportunities."

The email chimed again. I hurried back to the bed and picked up the laptop. The person had already responded to my email.

"Mom! Listen." I read to her. "'Etta: I am so sorry for the confusion; I was on the phone with someone named Sarah while I was writing the email to you. Apologies.'"

"Everyone is busy," Mom said. "Agents and editors go with what they think is right. That's all anyone can do. I'm just an American living in Europe writing about kids traveling. And right now some people don't want to travel. Personally, I would rather build bridges than walls."

"Do you think your stories scare people?"

"Because I'm not afraid of other people and cultures?"

"Yeah, I mean maybe that's why they don't like them."

"It's a story," she said. "Fiction helps us understand real life."

"Yeah, but–but–" I stammered, "you said it your-self that if people traveled more they wouldn't be so afraid of other people and the world would be a better place."

"I still believe that," she said. "And I always will."

Eiffel

Dad called from the kitchen. "Antoine is here."

Munda came in pushing a wheelchair and Mom sat, then whispered something to Munda.

"I'll take care of it," Munda said. "You have a great day with your family."

Antoine was waiting by the curb. He wore a black suit, and his hair was slicked back. He kissed everyone on both cheeks and opened the van's sliding door.

"La Tour Eiffel?" he asked, starting the engine.

"No," my mother said. "Drive around for a minute, please."

"The treasure hunt?" Antoine said, looking at Mom in the rearview mirror.

"Just the ones in central Paris, Antoine," she said with a wink.

"Treasure hunt?" I asked while Dad and I looked at Mom for an answer.

Mom stared out the windshield. "It's a secret!"

After we had driven around for a few minutes, she said, "Let's get some coffee. Shall we?"

"To a café, therefore?" Antoine asked, craning his neck back to us.

Mom was still in charge. "Let's go to one of the cafés in the Champs de Mars."

Moments later Antoine parked on a side street near the Eiffel Tower. He and Dad helped Mom into the wheelchair, and gravel crunched under the tires as we strolled down a long pathway. It was a perfect spring day, and the flowers and trees were blooming.

We sat at an outside table and the sun was shining through the trees and the light flickered on Mom's face.

"You look beautiful today," Dad said to Mom.

"Thank you," she said. "I love you."

"I love you, too."

I ordered hot chocolate and a chocolate croissant, and Dad, Antoine, and Mom had coffees.

When we left the café, Dad started pushing Mom in the wheelchair while Antoine made a phone call. In a few minutes, two security guards in green fatigues greeted us as we approached the tower. Huge black guns draped over their shoulders.

"These guards will escort you from here," Antoine said. "I will wait in the car."

With the soldiers leading us, we cut diagonally across the area in front of the Eiffel Tower and bypassed hundreds of tourists waiting in line.

At the entrance, one of our soldiers spoke to the security officer in a white short-sleeve shirt. This man quickly scanned us with a metal-detector wand and that was it. We were in. We didn't pay or wait or anything. In a few minutes, Dad, Mom, and I were in the elevator going to the second level. A man in a blue jacket met us when the door opened. His name tag read GUSTAVE, which I thought was perfect for someone at the Eiffel Tower.

"Follow me, please," Gustave said.

He led us to another elevator.

"Security regulations," he said, "prevent the use of wheelchairs on the top floor, madame. Should you wish to continue, you may do so with the aid of your cane. I will keep your wheelchair for you here, if you like."

Dad helped Mom stand while Gustave took the wheelchair, and the elevator door opened. It was oddly quiet. We were heading to the top of the Eiffel Tower. Just me and Mom and Dad.

And . . . an old man sitting on a stool in the corner. He was snoring with his mouth wide open. His hat seemed to keep him balanced as the elevator jiggled up to the top floor.

"Does he work here?" I asked in a whisper.

Dad said, "Maybe someone forgot him on the elevator."

The three of us giggled.

Then Mom leaned over her cane and began coughing loudly, her face turning bright red.

Dad put his arm around her. "Are you okay?"

"Yeah." She burped. "I think I had too much coffee."

She stepped back and held her arms in the air.

Then she ripped a huge burp that lasted at least thirty seconds. I couldn't believe it. It was embarrassing and hilarious.

Mom giggled. "Excuse me?"

Dad laughed and waved his hands. "That smells awful!"

"I'm so sorry." Mom nodded with a smile. "But I feel better!"

The old man snored loudly.

Mom, Dad, and I lost it. We were still cracking up when the doors opened on the top floor. It felt so good to be laughing.

Dad said, "Hope someone gets the old fella before we get back on."

"I hope they fumigate it!" Mom said. "Cancer and coffee is a bad combination. I'm sure burping is not allowed in heaven. They have strict environmental laws up there."

"Woman," my father said, jokingly. "You are a rare breed. Not many people talk about burping in heaven!"

We cracked up again.

"I'd rather laugh than cry," Mom said.

Dad turned and walked toward a tourist telescope. "I'm going to see if I can spot Henry in the apartment."

Mom held my hand.

"Being up here," I said, "reminds me of your books."

She looked right at me. "You do whatever you want with those stories. Okay?"

"Okay."

"And, be patient with your dad. Okay, Ellie?"

"Okay."

Mom gave me a hug. "I can see what you're thinking," she said. "I'll always be your mother. I'll always be with you. Like your friend Vicky says, together, forever."

Mom's stomach grumbled and she burped again.

"Mom!"

"This is awful, but the coffee was so worth it!"

Using her cane, Mom pointed at Dad, who was now looking through the telescope.

"Look how goofy your father is," she said. "He will need help when you move. He's spatially challenged."

"What?"

She grinned. "That means he doesn't know how to put furniture in a room. He understands financial markets, money, property, but when it comes to where the couch goes or how high the painting on the wall should hang, the man is clueless."

"I'll remember."

Dad snapped a few pictures of Mom and me as he walked back to us.

"You know," Dad said, pointing toward our apartment. "From up here it looks like Henry could fit an entire bedroom out on that balcony. I don't know why we're so crammed into the living room."

Mom and I looked at each other as Dad tried to explain how to furnish a balcony no bigger than a bathtub.

We giggled like friends, and I felt like everything was going to be fine.

"I think it's time to go," Mom said. "I believe this has been the best day of my life."

Wedding Ring

Munda had another curry dinner ready for us when we got back home. Mom went straight to her room, and Munda followed. Dad sat at his desk and spoke with Henry.

Munda came back out. "Ellie," she said. "Your mother is wanting to see you before she goes to bed."

There was something in Munda's voice that made me pause.

"Go on and get now, girl," Munda said. "Say good night to your mama. She's tired."

With her arm draping over the railing, Mom pushed the tilt button on her bed, and it buzzed up.

She yawned. "Hand me that box from the top dresser drawer."

I walked through the jungle of houseplants and stopped at the dresser. The collection of photographs framed Mom's life. I pulled on the drawer and took out the box.

"Open it," she said.

I cracked the lid and saw a ring shining right at me.

"That was my wedding ring."

"Is." I corrected her.

"*Is* my wedding ring," she said, taking it out of the box. "I want you to have it."

Her hand was shaking when she passed it to me. It had a big diamond in the center, surrounded by green stones.

"These are emeralds, aren't they?"

"Those are champagne-green sapphires, and the base is white gold. It's my ring and I want it to be yours."

"Mom," I said. "I can't wear this!"

"I haven't gone loopy on you yet, Ellie. It was my grandma Etta's ring. And since you both have the same name, I figured you could have it."

"Mom!" I said, sitting down on the bed next to her. "My name's Ella. Not Etta. Are you sure the medicine's not making you feel lightheaded?"

"You know what I'm talking about," she said softly. "You were supposed to be Etta."

"Tell me the story again."

She smiled.

I knew the story, but to hear it again would give me more time with Mom, *and* it was one of my favorites. I sat next to her, and Mom closed her eyes and started her tale.

"You were supposed to be named the fifth Etta in a line since my great-grandmother," she said. "At the hospital, when the nurse was writing your name on the birth certificate, you suddenly screamed from your crib. The nurse jumped, and everyone in the maternity ward ran over to see what was wrong. You just wanted some attention, or maybe you wanted to have a say-so in your name. The nurse who had been filling out the paperwork had only written Ella and had forgotten to cross the two *l*'s to make them into *t*'s. So instead of saying Etta, your birth certificate read Ella, and that's been your name ever since."

"Funny," I said.

Mom grinned. "Odd, how sometimes the smallest of things can have the biggest impact on your life."

I fell on her shoulder, and she wrapped her arms around me like I was a four-year-old. I must have drifted off because when I opened my eyes, I had been drooling.

She touched my cheeks. "No matter where I am," she said, "I will always be in your heart. Okay?"

"Okay."

She looked right at me. "I love you," she said. Then she held up two fingers and said, "Together." Then she raised four fingers. "Forever."

As I was leaving the room, she stopped me. "Be sure to give the ring to your father and tell him to put it in a safety deposit box for you, for when you need it."

I stared at the ring for a moment.

"Good night, Mom."

"Good night, sweetie," she said. "Oh, before you go, hand me my laptop."

"Why?"

 106

"It was such a good day that I feel like writing."

"You're tired."

"I am," she said. "I just need to do one thing."

I set the laptop on her bed.

"Ellie," she said.

"What Mom?"

"I love you."

"I love you too, Mom. Together. Forever."

En Berne

Sometime during the night Mom died. Or maybe it was that morning or the next day or the next week. I'm not really sure. It was kind of a blur for a while. A clock struck a point in time, and my mother, Etta Ashton Kerr, was not there, or anywhere, anymore.

I was walking down the stairs in pajamas, and Dad was standing at the door talking to a man in a white jumpsuit. Dad said good-bye and closed the door. He was wearing jeans and a white T-shirt and flip-flops. His eyes were red and watery, and I stood on the bottom step while he opened his arms and hugged me.

And I knew.

"I don't know how to tell you," Dad said.

He paused like the words were stuck in his throat.

"She's gone," he said. That's all he could say. "She's gone."

My eyes closed, and everything went blank. I seemed to fall down, down a deep well, but it was too dark to see anything. There was nothing left.

I knew my mom had been sick and might not make it, but then, when it really happened, it hurt much more than I ever thought it would.

That's the truth. Mom. My mom. My mother has really died. I couldn't believe it. It was the only thought I had.

Maybe they're just thoughts and not real. Like a book. Fiction. I have a bad novel in my head. That's what it is. Moms don't die. Right? I stood there on the step, hugging my father, and I searched my mind, hoping to find another story.

Open your eyes and everything will be fine, I told myself. *Maybe I can turn back the pages in this awful book and go back to the section on the Eiffel Tower where Mom and I are laughing at my goofy dad.*

This was a first. It was the first day knowing I'd never see my mother again. Ever again. I used to say, "My mom is a writer, even though nothing has been published." Now what was I supposed to say? "My mom *was* a writer? What would I say, now?"

Dad sat on the step and held me in his lap. I just sat there in his arms, waiting for Mom to come back. I didn't cry, at least not at first. I just tried to figure out what "gone forever" really meant. It made me numb.

My mind drifted into a dream, and I pretended this was the part in the movie called *My Life* where fairies fly into the scene and sprinkle stardust over the apartment and Mom's alive again, and the family lives happily ever after, just like in the tales. I listened for the fairies' wings flapping, but none came.

I cried for my mother who had died somewhere in the night in a room filled with plants and flowers.

It had happened while the Eiffel Tower flashed its lights, and the sweepers swept the streets of Paris and cleaned the city by lamplight, and the cafés and restaurants sent the stragglers home, and the bakers began to bake bread for another day, and the sun rose again, just like always. But on this day my mom was gone, gone forever.

I really couldn't believe what had happened.

There came a knock at the door.

"Bonjour?" It was Jean-Claude, the baker from downstairs. "Monsieur Kerr? Ellie?"

Dad opened the door, and the smell of fresh croissants filled the apartment.

"Bonjour, Jean-Claude," Dad said in a flat voice.

"Munda told me," he said. "I am very sorry for your loss."

The floral-shop woman walked in with an armful of flowers.

More and more people started coming by.

Later that morning, I stepped outside and spotted Alexa, Ji Yoon, and Bella walking hand in hand toward our house. In the square in front of our apartment building, Munda and Henry were talking to the woman at the stationery shop where Mom bought school supplies. The French flag and the American flag were hanging outside her door, and they were wrapped in black bands. Just like Dad had explained, the flags were *en berne* for when someone important dies.

To me, it seemed like the whole world was sad.

 110

Père Lachaise

For three days after Mom died, Munda, Dad, and I entertained people coming into the apartment. Jean-Claude brought fresh bread every day, and Dad's business friends stopped by, while Antoine played the cello. My mother had grown up in New Orleans, where they have parties and jazz bands at funerals and people celebrate the next part of life.

On the third day, Antoine came to the apartment to pick us up.

Mom had planned everything for her own funeral, which for her, was very normal.

Just before we left the apartment, the florist gave us girls each a bouquet of flowers.

Antoine and Dad wore dark coats with no ties and blossoms pinned to the lapels. I climbed into the back of the van with Munda, Bella, Alexa, and Ji Yoon.

Alexa and I were wearing matching brown sleeve-less dresses. Bella, with her long ponytail, wore a black skirt and blouse. Ji Yoon dressed in a white Korean robe, and Munda decorated herself in a multicolored gown with gold bracelets and necklaces.

Antoine drove the minivan to the most famous

cemetery in Paris, Père Lachaise. It was a place where famous people like Balzac, Chopin, and Jim Morrison were buried. We walked through the park down its windy stone lanes, past what seemed like miles and miles of gray tombs shaped like tiny houses, and came to the crematorium chapel.

The inside of the church was chilly and smelled dusty, but sunlight danced through the stained glass windows, making it feel warm. Rows of empty wooden chairs lined both sides of the aisles. People roamed quietly, lighting candles in the dark. Some carried little wooden boxes. In the ceiling, tiny tiles made a picture of the night sky, and the candlelight made the gold flecks in the mosaic sparkle like stars. At the far end of the chapel, where the altar would normally be, a priest was waiting for us.

Dad said Mom's name to the priest, and an altar boy came out from behind a velvet curtain, carrying a small wooden box.

The priest made the sign of the cross over the box and began saying a prayer. "Ashes to ashes. Dust to dust."

The priest handed the box of Mom's ashes to my dad. Then Antoine handed me an envelope and told me to open it.

"What is that?" Bella whispered.

"It looks like a treasure map," I said. "And there's a note."

"Your mother left you a map?" Ji Yoon asked.

"Posthumously," Dad muttered.

"What's that mean?" Alexa said as I unfolded the note.

"*Posthumous* comes from Latin," my father, the walking Wikipedia, explained to us. "*Post* means after. *Humus* means earth. *Humare* is the verb to bury. So *posthumous* means after the burial or after death."

"So it's a message?" Bella asked.

"Girls," Dad said. "Ellie's mother was different in many ways. I think it's her way of saying good-bye."

"We don't do that in South Korea," Ji Yoon said.

"I don't think it's done anywhere," Dad said.

"No," Munda said. "This is Etta Kerr. This does not surprise me at all."

"So what do we do?" I asked.

"Read the note," Antoine said, nodding his head like he knew exactly what the letter said. "I think she has something planned for you."

"The note reads," I said, "'Break on through to the other side.'"

Munda looked at us girls and shrugged.

"We don't get it," I said, speaking for the girls.

"That's a Doors song," Dad said, figuring out the clue. "It's a rock-'n'-roll band."

"Yeah, Mom told me," I said. "The 'people are strange' group."

"Exactly," Dad said. "The lead singer of the band was Jim Morrison, who died in Paris and is buried here in this cemetery."

"Then," Antoine said, "maybe we should go to his tomb."

"This is weird," Alexa said, letting her bouquet fall to her side.

"It is," Dad said. "I think when people have a crisis in their lives, like cancer, they become even truer to themselves. Things come into perspective. You kids knew my wife, and you know that she was all about laughing and having fun and traveling. I think this must be her farewell trip."

We followed Antoine across Père Lachaise Cemetery, down the stone paths, and around the tombs covered in old postcards. Some of the iron gates of the little stone houses were broken, and Ji Yoon, Alexa, Bella, and I peeked inside.

On the floors there were cracked picture frames, and, in some tombs, dusty plastic flowers in vases. In that moment by myself, I took a long breath and felt my heart sink. I think I was mostly sad that my mother wasn't there with us on this tour she had created.

A little while later we passed rows of tulips growing in a patch of green grass. The crowds started to get bigger. The sun broke through the trees, and Antoine stopped at a line of metal police barricades that encircled a cluster of tombs. In the middle of four little stone houses there was a small grave on the ground and a sign that read JAMES DOUGLAS MORRISON. People were everywhere, taking photographs, and a few were crying. One guy played a small guitar.

Bella spotted it first. "Look," she said. "There's a bundle of flowers tied to that barricade."

Ji Yoon said, "Just like ours."

Holding the box of Mom's ashes, Dad looked like he was holding back tears.

Antoine untied the new bouquet and handed it to Munda, and she poked around the flowers and pulled out a note.

"Deary," she said, handing me the message. "This must be for you."

Bella, Alexa, and Ji Yoon looked over my shoulder as I read, "'This place is a mountain for martyrs.'"

"What's *martyrs*?" Ji Yoon asked.

"A martyr," Alexa said, "is a victim, who suffers and dies."

"And," Dad added, "martyrs are people who give themselves up for a cause, for something they believe in."

"So," Ji Yoon said, "*martyr* is like Montmartre where Sacré-Coeur is."

I looked at Dad to confirm. "Mom planned a scavenger hunt for her funeral?"

"Apparently!" Antoine said. "Looks like we have our next stop."

We drove up to Montmartre, where my mother liked to go to church. When we got there, a nun on a bike gave us the next note. The nun was right out of one of Mom's books. This note sent us to the Palais-Royal, where we stopped in a café and had hot chocolate. When the waiter gave us the bill, it had a note written on the back.

It read, *The Rite of Spring*.

"It's a musical piece," Dad explained as he took the wooden box from the table, setting it in his lap, "written by Igor Stravinsky."

"Like the fountain," Ji Yoon said.

"The fountain?" Bella asked.

"Yes," I said. "At the Pompidou Centre!"

That was our cue, and we were off again. The whole day went like that. It was a tour of Paris. But our stops didn't seem to have any real meaning except a treasure hunt of sorts.

I heard Dad up in the front seat say to Antoine, "This is a little out of sequence, isn't it?"

Right then I realized Mom hadn't just made a scavenger hunt so that her funeral would be easier on me. She was also sending me a sign. We were following in the footsteps of the characters from her book series. That's why she had asked Ji Yoon's and Bella's and Alexa's parents if only the children could come to her service. Mom's funeral had copied a story she had written for children! She was taking us on the very same path that her characters had taken in her book. I couldn't help but think that it was a pretty creative idea, even if it was a memorial.

But as Mom used to say, I am biased.

Seeing the moon in the daytime was sort of odd. But as the day ended, the moon, full and white, began to hang low in the sky like a giant tear ready to drop.

Antoine stopped the minivan on an island in the middle of Paris. He took his cello from the back and led us to the railing overlooking the river. There were boats on the water and in the distance stood the Eiffel Tower. Ji Yoon, Bella, Alexa, and Munda and I stood in a half circle with our bouquets in hand.

Antoine started playing a mix of songs on the cello. He played the tunes of "Keep on the Sunny Side," "The Rite of Spring," and "Break on Through (To the Other Side)."

The wind started to blow just as the sun set, and Antoine changed to a song I didn't know. A deep, sad sound.

Dad stood on a bench in front of us with the box of ashes in his hands. He opened the wooden box, and Mom's ashes swirled up into the air like a tiny whirlwind wandering on its own.

"Good-bye, Etta," he said with a lump in his throat. "I love you."

Munda plucked a flower from her bouquet, and Ji Yoon, Alexa, Bella, and I did the same. Then we tossed the bundles of flowers up into the air.

Mom was a writer, an artist, and at that moment it felt like all the writers and artists in all the cafés in the whole city cried for her too.

Our bouquets floated up and the flowers broke

apart and a wind lifted the petals into the air and mixed them in with the ashes, and some rained down to the river while others drifted away.

I turned twelve that summer—my first birthday without my mother.

At some point after that, the movers came to pack up the apartment and take everything to America. I sat on the balcony and watched our belongings going out the front door.

I still couldn't believe it. My mom had died.

"She's gone?" I said to Dad. "Forever?"

"Yes," Dad said. "Forever."

Back in the States

"Forever?" I said, staring at Mom's locked laptop.

Outside I could hear Cookie and the American movers laughing again.

"Forever," Dad said. "The stories would be permanently gone."

He picked up the empty ashes box and looked at it. "We're moving into a new house and this is a new life for us. . . . Things may be a little unsettled for a while."

I nodded. "I miss Mom."

"I do too," he said. "But as Munda would say, we always have your mother's spirit with us."

"And her stories," I said. "She'll live forever if I can get those stories published. She'll be immortal!"

"True, in a sense," he said. "If you can figure out the password to her computer."

Outside my father's room, Cookie smacked on her gum. With her baseball cap on backward, she tapped on the wall. Behind her two of the movers were carrying Mom's dresser.

"Excuse me! Mr. Kerr," Cookie said. "Where d'you want this here chest of drawers?"

"Right there is fine," he said, staring at the ashes box.

"In the doorway?" she asked.

The men chuckled and set the dresser down, and everyone looked at Dad like he was nuts.

"What?" he said. "I don't know where the chest of drawers is supposed to go."

"Dad! It's obvious. It goes right there!" I said, pointing. "It's fine if you just put it against that wall, please."

Dad and I got out of the way so the men could get into the room. Now that Mom was gone, he was even more out of sorts. Mom had always said he wasn't the best at arranging furniture. Instead of Dad directing the movers, Cookie and I took charge.

Mom had been right. Dad would need a lot of help setting up the new house. A lot. The movers put the dresser down right where I had suggested.

"Ellie," Dad said. "That box right there at your feet has Mom's picture-and-mirror collection in it. If you want to set it up again, that would be a big help."

I set up the frames just like I had when Mom moved into her new room in our apartment back in Paris.

"So where does the ashes box go?" Dad asked.

"Duh!" I said. "It goes on the bookshelf."

"What do you mean, 'duh'?"

"Mom was a writer, Dad."

"Sorry, I'm thinking about something else."

I turned. "Dad, you do think Mom wants me to get her books published, *right*?"

"If *you* think she wants you to, then you should. You still have to have the password to get the stories."

"I'll figure it out."

He handed me a wrapped package.

"What's this?" I said.

"It's a present."

"I can see that," I said. "But what for?"

"I don't have anyone else to give gifts to."

I tore the paper.

"It's actually a souvenir I got for your mother, for her collection," Dad said. "Since you're setting it up now, I guess it's an appropriate time to add to it."

It was a frame of the Eiffel Tower made of tiny mirrors, and in the middle was the picture Dad had taken of Mom and me at the Eiffel Tower. I hugged Dad and held on tight. After I wiped my eyes, I put the frame on the dresser with the others.

"I wish Munda could see this."

"Me too," Dad said. "But she's going to be studying medicine for a long time."

"Why doesn't she go to school here? They have medical schools in the US. And you could help pay for it if she came here."

He shrugged. "Medical school is a lot of dough."

"Mom would want Munda here."

He smiled. "She certainly would."

Moving

Dad put on his running shoes and kicked his other shoes into the closet. "You know school starts next Monday," he said.

"I hate Mondays," I said.

I wasn't ready to start school, and secretly I was happy I had an entire week to find the password to Mom's computer. I planned to print the stories and take them to school on the first day.

"I need to get school supplies."

"Can't you just order it all online?"

"What if they run out of school supplies?"

"Ellie! The Internet is not going to run out of things to sell," he said. "I need to go for a run before I do anything. Why don't you go clean up your room?"

"There's nothing in there," I snapped. "There's only a lamp with no shade and a bed with no sheets."

He nodded like he had an idea. "That's what we need!" he said. "Sheets! We need to find sheets first."

"Sheets would be good," I said. I crawled up onto his mattress and grabbed the computer. "I wish Mom was here."

"Me too," he said. "Will you find the sheets, please?"

"I just want to figure out this password."

I opened the laptop.

"Try City of Light," he said.

"What?"

"The password," he said. "Try City of Light—Paris's nickname. Mom loved Paris. Right? Maybe she changed the password. Maybe she was delirious and didn't even know what she was doing."

"Maybe she did know," I said. "Maybe she was sending me a sign?"

"I don't know," he said. "Try anything, but be sure to power it down after the third failed attempt or you'll destroy all the data."

While I tried different passwords, Dad went for a run.

I wasn't going to take any chances. I would try only *two* passwords and then quit. I typed *CITYOFLIGHT*, and I tried *cityoflight*, and then I hit the power button and rebooted. I wrote the names frontward and backward. I even tried it in French: *villedelumiere*. Nothing. I worked on that stupid computer password for hours, typing anything that came to mind. I must have put in a million different codes.

All wrong.

About dinnertime, the movers finished bringing in the last few boxes, and Dad signed the papers with Cookie.

She winked at me and whispered, "You take care

of your daddy. I don't think he knows where anything goes!"

Dad and I continued opening boxes and putting things on the shelves. It was like a birthday. I'd tear into a box, and there would be a stuffed animal with a kitchen plate and some toothpaste. It was kind of fun. It was like getting a gift that you'd already gotten.

Mom (and Cookie) were right about Dad. He really was spatially challenged and didn't know where anything was supposed to go.

I knew things were bad when I saw him put the knife set in the fridge. Without Mom around, he was more trouble than help. It was like having a little brother who messed up your room once you got everything in the right place. Dad unpacked the plates and glasses and then put them in the cabinets in the laundry room. Of course I had to move them to the cabinets in the kitchen. He hung our nice paintings out in the garage, and I moved some back into the living room, where he hung them way too high on the walls. This was how it was going. So about halfway through the first week, I had had enough.

"Dad," I said, standing in a pile of wadded-up packing paper. "Why don't you just open the boxes and unwrap everything and I will come by and put things where they belong?"

"It's that bad?" he asked, knowing the answer.

I nodded.

"Okay," he said. "You're in charge."

His brain seemed muddled. Maybe he missed Mom or maybe it was the fact that his twelve-year-old daughter was now bossing him around. Whatever it was, he looked lost and probably needed to go to work.

Every night we ordered pizza or sushi, and we sat at the table with the candles lit like we used to. I peppered him with questions that might give me a clue for the password. This is where Dad was a master. His brain was like a search engine. He rattled off lists of everything, and I took notes until the candles burned out.

In the mornings, Dad opened a couple of boxes and went to work for a few hours. I got up and started putting things away. Each time I came across a book, I thought about Mom, and immediately I'd run over to the laptop and try some new passwords. I used foods, drinks, cities, songs, islands, planets, everything. I input the character names from her book series. I used my name, Mom's name, Dad's name, and even my friends' names. I think I tried all the titles of Shakespeare, Jane Austen, and Virginia Woolf. I even put in lines from songs and movies.

I came across a book of poetry and typed in parts of poems my mother liked. I used famous first lines like Maya Angelou's *But a caged bird stands on the grave of dreams* and Robert Frost's *Two roads diverged in a yellow wood.*

The poetry led me down a path but in the end I still hadn't found the password.

First Day of School

The first day of school was like . . . like . . . the first day of school anywhere in the world.

Even though the Grassland School was only three blocks from my new house, I rode in the car with Dad on his way to work. A few school buses turned in to the drop-off line, and a clump of girls with backpacks walked across the park. Three boys on bikes ran the stop sign in front of us, and a traffic policeman whistled at them.

Grassland took up a whole city block with its new buildings that overlooked a perfectly designed lacrosse-and-soccer field. The playground looked brand-new with swinging bridges and spiral slides. The bushes and trees were trimmed, and the side-walks had no cracks.

When I got out of the car, I looked at my reflection in the window. I was wearing my new favorite floral blouse that Mom had picked out for me in France. I checked my hair, and that's when I saw the look on Dad's face. He was crying. Then he smiled at me.

He mouthed, "I love you."

And I mouthed back, "I love you, too."

The guard blew a whistle at us, signaling my dad to keep moving through the drop-off line. As he drove away, it really hit me. Without my mom, I wasn't ready for anything.

Students at the American School of Paris were used to being the new kids. They were not only from other schools, but from other countries! At the Grassland School that year, there was only one new kid in sixth grade.

Moi—just me.

Seeing my dad crying was a shock, but it also made me think of Mom, which made me smile because she'd told me that we would always be together, forever. I decided to keep on the sunny side, and I opened the gate.

As I stepped onto the school grounds, I felt like everyone was watching me. My backpack suddenly felt extra heavy.

Does anyone know about my mother? Do they know I moved from Paris? Will anyone even care?

I had to act normal.

Again Mom saved me. She used to tell me that you can only make a first impression once. I smiled as I scanned the faces staring at me from the playground. I knew I wouldn't see anyone I knew. When you don't know anyone, everyone looks almost the same. To me, they were all new.

Then I recognized someone.

Actually, it was a hairdo that was familiar. Spiky

blond hair. I stared at the boy. *Why do I know him?* Since we had moved, I had been inside my house pretty much the whole time, unpacking and looking for the password. I couldn't possibly know anyone. The only people I had seen were the pizza man, the sushi chef, and the movers.

And . . . the kid on the bike. Pete. Pete Morgan.

He fixed his backpack on his shoulders and approached. But not too close. He seemed shorter now that he wasn't on a bike. I decided to be nice and break the ice.

I thought being concerned about his almost accident would be a good place to begin.

"Hey," I said, "aren't you the boy that almost wrecked into our moving truck?"

He tucked his chin in. "No," he snapped. "I didn't almost wreck. I meant to go up the ramp. It's a trick bike, you know."

"You were lucky you didn't hit the truck."

"I wasn't staring at you."

"I didn't say you were."

We had gotten to "awkward" very quickly.

Just then a bigger kid walked up and stood behind him.

"Hey, Pete," the boy said. "You already got a new girlfriend on the first day of school?"

"Be quiet, Marcus," Pete said. "I'm not Justin, you know."

"I am not his girlfriend," I said. "I just moved here."

"Oh yeah, from where?" Marcus said.

In the short amount of time that it took us to have this little conversation, a full-blown crowd had gathered around. Everyone was watching me. The whole school knew I was there. And the one question on everyone's mind was: Where did she come from?

A cloud of silence covered the entire schoolyard, or at least it seemed that way to me. The little kids who were playing on the jungle gym stopped. The swings slowed to a sway. The older kids sitting under a big tree went silent. A huge group of what looked like sixth-grade girls focused only on me. I imagined teachers looking out classroom windows waiting to see what the new kid might do.

My answer to Marcus's question had to be perfect. Then it hit me.

The Foreigner

As I stood there, I could feel my mother's voice filling my heart. *Be kind and put your best foot forward.*

I just wanted to be honest without seeming stuck-up. Haughtiness on day one will stay with you forever. If I said "France," it would sound like I was trying to one-up everyone. My answer had to be truthful yet something we all had in common, and my tone had to be perfect, too—it had to sound . . . normal.

I went with nonchalant casual and made it seem like not a big deal. "I just moved here from . . ." I paused. "From an American school."

Pete and Marcus nodded as if my answer were good enough. It was honest and not super clear, but it had worked, at least for a moment.

As the news of my response slowly spread across the school grounds, everyone seemed satisfied and went back to what they had been doing. The swings cranked up again. The little kids on the jungle gym started climbing and sliding, and the older students under the tree returned to chatter.

A dozen kids, however, swarmed around me like some odd bird had just flown in.

"So," Pete asked, "where was the American school?"

"In the suburbs of Paris," I said.

"France?" Marcus asked.

"Yes."

"Cool," they both said at the same time.

A voice from the back of the group spoke up. *"Parlez-vous français?"*

The person was asking me if I spoke French.

Again, I couldn't seem like a know-it-all.

The crowd split, with the girls moving to one side and Marcus and Pete and the boys on the other. I could now see who it was. It was a kid with slicked-back hair, wearing holey jeans, a shirt open halfway, and a gold necklace bobbing on his tan chest. He was leaning over his bike's handlebars. Fortunately, Mom's voice came to me. *Be kind.*

Instead of responding in French, I simply said, "Yes, I do speak French."

Marcus said, "Whoa, I didn't know Justin spoke French!"

Justin rolled his bike through the middle of the group and pointed at me with both hands in a pistol shape.

He said, "My mom told me we had a French kid this year." He looked me up and down. "So I guess you're it?"

"I'm not French," I said. "I just went to school in France."

"Ooh la la," he said.

Marcus snickered, and Justin gave Pete a high five.

If this kept up, it was going to be a long day. I looked at the girls, hoping they would save me from Justin's injustice. Luckily, a girl stepped forward and spoke up.

"So what's your name, anyway?" she said in a kind voice.

"I'm Ellie."

"I'm Malia," she said. "Is that where you got that blouse? In Paris?"

"Yeah," I said, glancing down at the shirt. "My mom got it in Provence, which is actually in the south of France."

"That is so cool," she said. "I want to learn another language too, 'cause I want to be an ambassador one day."

I was so excited that someone was interested in traveling like I was. "Diplomats and expats have really nice houses," I said. "And you can go everywhere in the world."

"What's *expat*?" Pete asked.

Before I could answer, Justin crossed his arms in the shape of an *X*. "A French video game," he said. "X-PAT."

The boys laughed and the girls ignored them. Malia gestured toward the girl next to her.

"Katie and I are both taking French this year," she said. "Maybe you could help us study."

"Do you really speak French?" Katie asked.

"I do."

This girl looked a little like Vicky from my old school but with pigtails and freckles.

Katie said, "My parents have been to France about a million times. I think it sounds like the best."

"I know more French," Justin interrupted. He stared right at me and said, *"Je t'aime."*

I was shocked.

Justin fiddled with his gold chain. "That means 'I love you.'" He cocked his head toward the boys. "I know the important words in French."

Malia said, "I'm already sick of you, Justin, and the first bell of the year hasn't even rung yet."

I was officially ready for school to start.

Justin was undeterred. "So what was the name of your school over there?"

A few teachers were cutting across the playground and heading toward the middle school building. First period couldn't be that much longer.

I said, "The school was called the American School of Paris."

"You're telling me that there is an American school in Paris like just for kids?"

"Yeah," said Malia answering the question. "There are hundreds of American and international schools all over the world for people who live outside of their home countries. Like for diplomats and ambassadors' kids."

"Well," Justin said, "my dad said that the French

don't ever support us, so we shouldn't support them."

"I don't know what you're talking about," I said. I could feel Mom's nerve in me. I had to defend myself and the friends that I had left in France. "Have you ever been to France?"

"No," he said.

"Has your dad?"

"No," he said, curling his lip. "He went to Canada once, and he said the signs on the highway were written in English and in French. Is that stupid or what?" He turned toward Pete and Marcus. "Everybody should just speak English."

"What if it's not your native language?" I asked.

"Ooh," Marcus said. "Burn!"

Justin barked. "Shut up, fatso."

"Hey, man!" Pete said. "You ought to be cool, Justin. Her mom died over there."

I blushed. "How did you know that?"

This was news I was *really* not ready to share. The girls stared at me.

"My mom told me," Pete said. "I wasn't supposed to say anything, was I?"

Justin slapped Pete in the chest.

Pete hung his head. "I always say the wrong thing at the wrong time."

An uncomfortable silence came over the group. I think they wanted to hear what I had to say about my mother, but I didn't want to talk about it right then.

Fortunately, the bell rang.

As the entire schoolyard moved toward the buildings, I could hear a pair of what sounded like clogs
clonking on the concrete behind me.

Pete and Marcus didn't look back. Justin ditched
his bike at the bike rack, and the boys took off running
straight for the middle school.

Malia, Katie, and I stopped and looked back.

It was the head of the middle school, Ms. Bean.
I'd seen her photograph, but she looked different in
person. She wore shoes that looked and sounded like
actual wooden clogs. Her dress was purple with frilly
white lace around the collar. She looked like she was
about three hundred years old.

"Girls!" Ms. Bean shrieked. "Just because you've
made friends with the new *international* girl does
not mean that we're going to have secret or foreign
languages spoken outside of the classroom. Is that
clear?"

I nodded heavily. For me, Ms. Bean was extra scary.
With her cat-eye glasses, she looked exactly like the
mean woman in Mom's stories.

The Road to Success

Homerooms should always have teachers who understand what home really means.

On that first day of school, Ms. Hart wore a dress with a huge sunflower on it. She had decorated the classroom in a vacation theme with pictures of exotic places hung in the corners of the room. There were trinkets and clothing from Asia, Africa, South America, Europe, and North America.

Written on the whiteboard was this message: *Keep vacation going by traveling with your imagination!*

I strolled into class with my brand-new friends—Katie and Malia—and took a seat near the front. Ms. Hart greeted us as she passed by.

"Bonjour," she whispered. "I am so thrilled to have you in my class!"

Right then I knew everything would be okay. If you have a good homeroom teacher, then the new-school blahs just fade away.

Even though it was the first day, Ms. Hart didn't mess around. Good teachers start teaching as soon as they can. One second after homeroom, she began. We had a STEAM schedule—science, technology, engineering, art, and math.

When something happens to you, good or bad, reminders of it seem to pop up everywhere. Like when your family gets a new car, you suddenly see the same kind of car everywhere. Or when you learn a new word, you start hearing it all the time.

Ms. Hart taught science, and in the very first lesson we studied the parts of a flower.

Flowers are a little like people. There are males and females, and like people they eventually fall in love and make new flowers. We learned about the stamen, with its anthers and filament. We drew pictures of the pistil with its stigma, style, and ovary. And there it was—a reminder of Mom and her ovarian cancer.

At lunch I met up with Malia and Katie and a few other girls. They made me feel not so alone. Eating lunch by yourself is the worst.

There were others who just had to say something to me. Between lunch and break, I stopped by my locker and a boy came up to me. His hair was so long on one side that I could only see one eye.

"You're lucky to have lived somewhere else," he grunted from behind the mop. "I wish I could leave. I hate it here."

And that was it. He walked off by himself.

Some kids thought it strange that I had lived in another country, but others thought it was cool. But Pete seemed most interested.

I spotted Pete swaying on an old swing set in the corner of the schoolyard. He waved me over, and since I didn't want to stand alone on the playground, I cut across the field and joined him.

We swung for the whole break, which was great because I was moving, and I felt better knowing the time was passing.

Pete was actually very nice. He asked me about where I had lived and about my school. I told him about our apartment and the Eiffel Tower and my friends in Paris. When Pete ran out of questions, he would swing higher.

On the way back to class, Malia, the future diplomat, caught up with me. Her eyes were big and round and her smile excited.

"Okay! If I were an ambassador," she said, "how would you introduce me in French?"

I said, "*Permettez-moi de vous présenter* . . . Malia."

"That's easy," she said. "Permit me to present to you . . . Malia."

"Exactly."

From somewhere down the hallway a pair of wooden clogs clonked toward us. Everyone looked around to see from which direction the sound was coming. I spun around. Over the sea of middle school heads, Ms. Bean curled a gnarly finger at Malia and me, signaling us to come and see her.

The kids between us scattered. For me, I was extra frightened. I was about to come face-to-face with what looked like, an evil character from my mom's book.

"Miss Kerr," she said to me. "Did I not make it clear to you this morning that I *prefer* foreign languages be spoken in foreign-language class and *not* secretively in the hallways?"

I nodded, hoping to end the lecture quickly.

"Let me set you straight from the get-go," she said. Then she stopped, raised her arm high in the air, and snapped her fingers so loudly I thought for a second my eardrum had burst.

Without taking her eyes off me, Ms. Bean pointed at the boy who had told me he hated school.

"Gavin Moss," Ms. Bean said. "Get that hair cut, young man and get to class!"

The boy shuffled down the hallway.

Then, looking at Malia, she said, "And you, Malia. You know the rules at this school, don't you?"

Malia nodded obediently and scurried off to class.

Ms. Bean came closer and towered over me. "Let's chat," she said.

I walked backward straight into her office. She closed the door, offered me a chair, and crabbed back around her desk, where she sat behind a stack of papers.

"So," Ms. Bean said, folding her arms, "that leaves me and you, Ella Elizabeth Kerr."

"I go by—"

"I know what you *go by*," Ms. Bean said. "I will call you by the name on your registration form. She tapped a piece of paper on her desk. "Is that clear?"

I nodded.

"I am very sorry to hear about your mother. That is dreadful news. We will do whatever is necessary to make you comfortable here at the Grassland School."

While she paused, I wondered if grown-ups went to special schools to learn how to say something without actually meaning it.

Ms. Bean leaned across the desk, bulldozing layers of paper with her hairy forearms. "I was going to go to Europe at one time myself, you know. Had a boyfriend. Ended up that he went and *I* couldn't. Travel is so enjoyable, yet there are some drawbacks to living outside of one's home culture."

I didn't know what she was getting at.

"I'm sure you've picked up some awful habits while at school in Europe," she said, glancing toward the window. "I've seen it time and time again. Kids not following the rules, flouting tradition, thinking they can do whatever they want."

Ms. Bean peered over the top of her cat-eye glasses. "Let me be clear. This. Is. My. School. And I run a tight ship. My philosophy is simple: We teach. You learn. Okay?"

She sat back and smiled like she was trying to be nice.

I breathed for the first time in a few minutes and tried to form a thought. Before I could say anything, she spoke again.

"Why can't you speak foreign languages in the hallways? Is that the question forming in your twelve-year-old brain right now? You see, I'm the teacher and the principal. I. Know. Things. I'll answer your question. We can't have foreign languages in the hallways because we've got to understand what everyone's saying. Okay? Spanish is for Spanish class. French for French class. In America and in my school, we speak English. American English. Period. Is that clear?"

I wanted to run away to a foreign country and never come back but decided instead to close my eyes.

"Ella?"

I opened my eyes and looked at her, partly thinking that I would see some dragon hissing fire at me.

"The road to success is lined with rules." She smiled broadly. "Follow the rules and you'll have a fantastic year."

Author, Writer

I decided I would avoid Ms. Bean all year.

As it turned out, the principal was, fortunately, the only person at the school who seemed sour about my living abroad. My teachers thought it was neat. And everyone was honestly sincere when they told me how sorry they were about my mother. That was really nice to hear.

School was still school. By the end of the week, the friend groups were fixed.

The Grassland School was my third school, and what was amazing to me was that kids in all my schools bunched together in basically the same type of clusters.

There were always the sports kids—mostly soccer, with boys and girls whose main desire was to kick a ball. It's all they did during the break. I love soccer (or football as it's called in Europe), but I didn't want to play it all the time. A few Grassland kids told me how awesome France's soccer team was, which was a nice thing to say.

In every school there was always one tough kid (or one who *acted* tough) and his gang. Justin played this role perfectly.

The nerds, like everywhere, were sort of . . . well . . . nerdy. Gavin, the guy with long hair on one side, fit into this group.

And every school had cliques that clumped together circling the campus. Grassland was no different.

I know these might be stereotypes, but for me it really was the same in the three schools that I had been to, even in two different states and two different countries.

Lastly, there were the stragglers. At this school these were Pete, Katie, Marcus, Malia, and me. We had no group. But for the first week of school we were never alone because all the stragglers met by the old swing set.

On Friday of this first week I met up with the "I don't have a group" group. Near the end of break, three girls were rounding the soccer field for the third time, and they decided to pay us a visit at the swings.

Brooklyn Alexis was the queen bee. She had long black hair and wore expensive name-brand clothes every day. The worker bees in this clique were two other dark-haired girls: Blaine and Paisley.

With her sidekicks buzzing at her flanks, Brooklyn planted herself in front of the swing I was sitting on. My friends froze.

She looked right at me. "I need some clarification."

"Okay," I said.

"I heard Ms. Bean say your real name was Ella,

not Ellie," Brooklyn said. "Is that like a nickname or something?"

I thought about telling her how I was actually supposed to be Etta. But I didn't want to share my story, and certainly not with her.

"Yeah," I said, "everyone just calls me Ellie."

Brooklyn sighed. "We were just trying to figure some things out," she said, looking at Blaine and Paisley. "For one, your name. Now we know: Ella is your name; Ellie is your nickname. Your mom's name, though, was Etta, right?"

"Yeah," I said hesitantly.

Marcus cleared his throat. "Why don't you mind your own business?"

"This *is* my business." Brooklyn shrugged. "Pete's mother told my mother that your mother was an author."

"She was," I said.

I glared over at Pete sitting on his swing, and he blushed.

"Well," Blaine said, tilting her head. "We looked up your mom's books on Amazon last night, and her name's not anywhere."

"Like nowhere," Paisley said. "No Etta, no Ella."

"You looked up my mom on Amazon?" I asked.

"Yeah!" Brooklyn huffed. "Like the biggest store, ever."

"That proves it," said Blaine.

Malia hopped off her swing. "Proves what?"

Brooklyn hooked her hair behind her ear. "I'm not trying to be rude, and I'm honestly really sorry about your mom and all, but I mean there's no author by the name of Etta Kerr. Right?"

"She—she never . . . ," I stammered. "My mom was never able to get her stories published."

Paisley said, "So, technically she wasn't an author?"

"Her mom was a writer," Katie said. "Author, writer—same thing."

Brooklyn batted her eyes. "My dad told me that to be an author you have to have a book published." She shrugged again. "Just sayin'."

Brooklyn Alexis was the queen bee for good reason. She certainly had my vote. She got under my skin that day so bad that I wanted to cry. But more than that, I just wanted her and her clique to go away.

And then the words just came out of my mouth.

"Okay," I said, "so if you have to be published first so you can be a writer–I mean an author–well, then, I'm going to get my mom's stories published."

Brooklyn looked puzzled. "And how are you going to do that, exactly?"

A Great Idea

The Brooklyn bees buzzed back to class.

I turned to my group on the swings.

"I need some help," I said.

Marcus stepped forward and folded his arms like he was standing guard. "With what?" he asked.

I told them the story about my mom and her cancer, and the stories she hadn't been able to get published. Once I had spilled the beans about my mom and our lives in France, I actually felt a lot better.

The gang stared back at me.

"So my mom's stories—the Explore the World series—are on a computer that is blocked by a password that was changed just before my mother died."

"You could hack into it," Malia said.

"Ask Gavin Moss," Katie said. "He's ridiculous with coding."

"Good idea," Pete said.

Katie whistled across the playground. "Gavin!" She signaled for him to come over.

As soon as Gavin shuffled up, I explained about the algorithms and the fact that if we got the password wrong four times in a row, everything would be deleted.

Gavin nodded. "Then three's the max."

Malia asked. "Can you hack into her computer?"

"Depends," Gavin said slowly.

"Can you?" Katie asked. "Or can't you figure out a password?"

"All passwords," Gavin said, "at some point need people—you know, human beings, living creatures—to decide what the code is. Typically in a situation of this sort, some of my white-hat hacking friends get together and brainstorm ideas, possible passwords, and strategies for attacking the system."

Pete pursed his lips. "Why don't we have a hacking party?"

"What do you mean?" I asked.

"We come over to your house," Pete explained, "and help Gavin and his friends hack into your mom's computer."

"Not at my house," I said. "No way."

"Why not?" Pete asked.

"Because our house is a wreck," I said. "My dad is spatially challenged."

"What?" Katie asked.

"That means he can't figure out where anything goes," I explained. "The first week we were here, we unpacked everything, and now we have stuff just sitting everywhere. Our kitchen is so disorganized you wouldn't believe. We don't even cook dinner. We eat pizza or sushi almost every night."

"Yum," Marcus said. "That sounds good to me."

Malia stepped closer. "You know, you could have a 'clean up the house' party while Gavin works on the computer."

"That's a great idea," Katie said. "My parents had a painting party at our new house."

"Nobody wants to do that," I said.

"I do," Pete said.

"Me too," Marcus said.

Katie nodded. "You know who we need?"

Malia, Marcus, and Pete all said at the same time, "Hannah!"

Katie yelled across the playground, and they waved Hannah over.

"What are you doing?" I asked.

"Trust us," Katie said.

Hannah left the girls she was talking to and skipped up to us at the swing set. Hannah had brown hair and a big smile. She was wearing a gray and black skirt with a fluffy red blouse. Very French. She was holding a phone tight in her hand.

"What's up?"

Pete said, "Ellie's going to have a party."

"I am not!" I said.

Malia ignored my comment. "The theme is 'Get Ellie's house in order!'"

"Yes!" Hannah said cheerfully. "I love to organize. I'm going to be a designer when I grow up. Can we paint?"

"No!" I said.

"My parents," Hannah said, "painted at Katie's parents' house party. They said it was a blast."

I stepped back. "I don't know if my dad will like this."

Malia said, "You mean your dad doesn't want you to straighten up the house? And make friends at the same time?"

"Well, I mean . . . of course he does."

"So when's the party?" Hannah asked.

"Tomorrow," Pete said. "It's Saturday. Let's do it tomorrow."

"I can't," I said. "My dad's going to a conference."

Malia asked, "And he's leaving you at home alone?"

"Just for the day," I said.

"Perfect," Katie said. "It'll be a surprise."

Hannah opened a planning app on her phone. "Works for me. I'm free all day tomorrow."

I had to admit that I kind of liked this idea, but still I was nervous. "I can't have a whole bunch of people hacking into my mom's computer."

"Why would they be doing that?" Hannah asked.

Malia answered, "Because we want to help Ellie get her mom's unpublished stories off a computer that's blocked by some cryptic password."

"Cool!" Hannah said. "You could publish them."

"Don't worry," Gavin said matter-of-factly. "I'll do the hack solo."

"And," Marcus said, "I can make breakfast while you guys are straightening up."

Pete said, "Marcus is a great chef!"

It was going to happen. Whether I wanted it to or not.

The Party

Dad left early the next morning before I woke. When I went into the kitchen, I found a note. It read: *Sorry the place is such a wreck. I'll make it up to you. Promise.*

Outside, a gang of kids marched toward my house. Pete was in front on his bike, followed by Katie, Hannah, and Malia. Gavin shuffled down the middle of the street, carrying two backpacks. Marcus pulled a wagon filled with grocery bags.

When they stepped into the house, no one said anything. They stood in the foyer next to a mattress wrapped in plastic and stared at the disaster that was my house.

"We can do this!" Pete announced with confidence. "Oh yeah!"

"This place is a wreck!" Hannah said.

I explained, "My dad's been a little mixed up since my mom."

"Where did you say your dad was going to be?" Hannah asked.

"At a conference," I said. "All day."

"Hannah," Katie said. "You are officially in charge."

"The way I see it . . ." Hannah folded her arms. "We have three goals."

I liked Hannah.

"Number one," she said. "We obviously have an organization problem here. Two, there's the issue of breakfast because I am *starving*! And three, the most important thing, the computer password, because I think we all really want to help Ellie get her mom's stories."

Everyone nodded.

Hannah pointed at Marcus. "You start making breakfast." She pointed at Gavin. "You said you'd work solo, so get on the computer and start hacking, or whatever it is you do."

I said to Gavin, "After the third failed password, you have to shut it down, or the data will be destroyed."

"Got it," he said.

Gavin sat at the dining room table and took computers and wires from his backpacks. Then he connected a bunch of cables to Mom's laptop and began working.

"Wow!" He mumbled to himself. "I've only read about homemade computers like this."

Marcus pulled his wagon of food into the kitchen.

Hannah scanned the room. "Pete, you and Malia take everything that doesn't belong in this room, like"—she tapped the mattress wrapped in plastic—"like this, and like that ladder on the fireplace." She opened the closet door. "And take these rakes and shovels to the garage."

Hannah scanned the room again. The decorator in her was kicking in. "Ellie, Katie, and I will work on getting this place looking like a home," she said. "Three main areas for us: cleaning, wall hangings, and furniture organization."

"I'll need a couple of hours," Gavin said, not looking up from his computer station. "This is amazingly cryptic!"

Hannah looked at Katie and me. "Okay, where are the cleaning supplies?"

"Look under my dad's bed," I said. "The room at the end of the hall."

"What?" Katie asked. "Never mind. I'll find them."

Pete and Malia moved the table saw into the garage, and Katie started cleaning the house. Hannah and I discussed where the furniture should go. By the time we were ready, Malia and Pete had finished moving out all the things that didn't belong.

Then we cranked. The four of us pushed rugs, couches, and tables into the right places. We rehung pictures and paintings. We came across lampshades and pillows and vases and books and found homes for them all.

Once we had completed a room, Hannah would come in and make sure everything was as she wanted it. The back of the house smelled like cleaning stuff. Katie even scrubbed our toilets! Now that's a real friend. The front of the house had a sweet scent of pancakes as Marcus's breakfast began to take shape.

No one talked. Everyone just worked.

Finally, things were where they belonged. The blender was in the kitchen and not in the bedroom. The tools were hanging in the garage. The shower had a curtain hanging instead of towels. There were even logs in the fireplace. It was a great house.

"Brunch is ready," Marcus called out.

Marcus was clearly a chef. He had set out an enormous spread of breakfast on the dining room table. There were pitchers of orange juice and apple juice, platters of bacon and sausage, mountains of pancakes and hash browns, scrambled eggs, eggs in a basket, croissants, syrup, honey, butter, jelly. Everything.

"Where did you get all of this?" I asked.

Marcus smiled. "My mom bought it for us this morning, for the party."

We sat down and ate and ate and ate.

At the other end of the table, Gavin tapped on the keyboard. "I can't get it," he muttered. "Somebody's even disabled all the function keys. There's no way to trick this computer."

"There's no trick," I said. "We just have to find the right password."

"I realize that," he said. "My password bot would take years to type in all the possible combinations."

"Let me try," Malia said, putting down her fork. "I'm going to be a diplomat or a spy. I should be able to crack codes."

For the next several hours we took turns trying

every password in the world. We ate so many pancakes that I thought we might have broken a Guinness World Record for the most eaten in one sitting.

But when everyone left, we were still missing the password.

Pete

Dad was so surprised by how neat and clean the house was that when he came home, he sprinted from room to room, gawking and pointing at everything. He opened the drawers and the cabinets, and finally he plopped down on the couch and folded his arms. I sat next to him.

"You are amazing," he said. "You've overcome a lot to do this." He gave me a hug and said, "Thank you. I love you."

With the house now in order, things at home started to settle down to normal.

Except for that stupid password.

The second week of school, I really started to miss living in Paris. At break I went to the swing set by myself, hoping no one would join me. Sometimes you just need to be alone. But this was the place where the solo kids met, so no one was ever alone, even when you really wanted to be.

Pete walked up. "What's up with you?"

"Nothing," I said.

"You look sad."

"I just want to be alone."

"Why'd you come here?" he asked.

"I didn't have any other place to go. I'm new. Remember?"

"Did you get the password?"

"No."

"Did you try again?"

"All day yesterday."

Pete sat on a swing and kicked his shoes in the dirt. We didn't say anything for a while. Then he planted his feet and twisted in the swing.

"Want to teach me French?"

"You don't want to learn French, Pete."

"Do too," Pete said. "Well, my mom and I were talking about you. Actually, I mean I was telling her about you at dinner. I mean, I was at dinner, talking about you and the party and all. But not in a bad way. I was just telling her—"

"Pete."

"I have trouble sometimes getting my words out. Ok-k-kay?" He stopped, like he had forgotten what he was asking.

"Why," I asked, "do you want to learn how to speak French?"

"Oh yeah," he said. "Because my dad used to speak French."

"Used to?" I asked, looking right at Pete. "Why doesn't he speak French anymore?"

"He died."

I froze and then finally said, "Are you serious? I am

so sorry. I didn't . . ."

I had been so focused on the loss of my own mother that I hadn't even taken the time to ask Pete about his family. It felt odd to be on the other side of someone else's sorrow.

"He had cancer too," Pete said. "Like your mom."

"What kind of cancer did your dad have?"

"S-something . . . ," he stuttered. "I don't know exactly. I was only like two years old when he died. What kind did your mom have?"

"It's called ovarian."

Pete's face went blank.

It was the first time I had spoken with another person about Mom's type of cancer.

He said, "I guess that's a pretty bad kind."

I nodded.

"Well . . . I don't really know," he stumbled. "I mean, maybe that's what my dad had too."

I laughed a little. "You don't know what *ovarian* is, do you?"

"It's a type of cancer?" he said like he was asking a question.

"Only women—girls, females—have ovaries," I explained. "You remember in Ms. Hart's class, on the first day of school when we drew the parts of a flower? Science class? The female part of the flower has ovaries, and that becomes the fruit. Ovaries help make babies. Females have ovaries. You don't have ovaries, Pete, and your dad didn't either."

Pete's face turned red, and he stabbed the toes of his shoes into the dirt. "I didn't really want to talk about that."

"Me either." I changed the subject, "Why don't you learn Spanish instead of French?" I asked. "There are tons of people who speak Spanish in the US."

"Exactly."

"Exactly what?"

"Hundreds of millions of people already speak it," he said. "Nobody speaks French. That would be cool. I don't always want to be like everybody else."

I liked Pete.

"Actually a lot of people speak French, but whatever," I said. "Let's start with hello." I cleared my throat and said, *"Bonjour."*

"Bonjour," Pete repeated.

"Good accent."

I moved onto the "my name is" lesson. *"Je m'appelle* Ellie," I said, pointing to myself.

Pete said with a dumb smile, *"Je m'appelle* Ellie."

"No, silly. I'm Ellie. You're supposed to say, 'I call myself Pete,' not 'I call myself Ellie'!"

Pete slapped his forehead and fell off the swing and into the dirt, where he cracked up. At the end of break we walked back into school, and he kept snickering and repeating to himself, *"Je m'appelle* Ellie!"

A Simple Solution to a Complicated Problem

Throughout the first semester, the "I don't belong to a group" group got a lot of new members. Every week new kids joined us. We would meet at break and after school when we didn't have a million things to do.

One day after school I was near the swing set by myself.

Pete came by and asked, "Password?"

I shook my head, and Pete dropped into a seat. It was late January, and the weather was cool but sunny. The sky was bright blue and patches of snow on the grass were melting. We talked about everything.

"When I was in France," I said, "I ate chocolate every day."

Pete spoke French. *"Chocolat,"* he said.

"That's awesome, Pete!" I said.

"Did you really eat chocolate every day?"

"Every day."

"You're lucky."

"You know what they say," I said. "When in Rome . . ."

"I thought you were in Paris?" Pete asked.

"It's an expression."

"I know," he said. "Just kidding."

Then he got a serious look on his face.

"Ellie?" he asked.

"Yes."

"Can I ask you a personal question?"

"That depends."

"Why don't you ever ride your bike to school?"

I smiled. "That's not personal, Pete!"

Pete seemed a little embarrassed.

I said, "I don't ride my bike because I live right on the other side of the park. It's just as easy to walk."

"Well . . ."

It seemed like he wanted to say something.

"What's bugging you?"

His head dropped. "Nothing."

"Are you still upset about that day you rode your bike up into our moving truck?"

"That's not funny."

"It was funny to the movers," I said.

He quickly changed the subject and said, "So when Justin said, *Je t'aime,*' to you that first day of school, um, does that really mean, 'I love you'?"

Pete glanced away, and suddenly something in my stomach felt different.

Pete had just repeated the three most spoken words in any language: *I. Love. You.* My mother had said the very same thing to me a million times. Those were the last three words I ever heard my mom say to me: *I love you.*

Wait, I thought. *Those weren't the last words she said to me.*

I flew off the swing. "I gotta go!"

I ran.

"Wait!" I heard Pete yell. "I didn't mean to say that! I was just . . ."

I didn't stop. I ran out the side gate of the school and sped home to the computer and the password that I knew I knew.

When You Know You Know

I didn't even close the front door I was going so fast. I ran inside the house, turned on Mom's computer, and waited for what felt like forever. The little blue lights scrolled around and around the screen. I think computers know when you're in a hurry, and they start slowly just to make you wait, just to test your patience. I had waited half a year to type in this password. It had been long enough.

The login screen on the laptop came up.

I typed in my mom's name and then *iloveyou.*

The computer made a sound. *Blip.*

The screen read THE USERNAME OR PASSWORD IS INCORRECT.

I thought about what had inspired me. Pete. He didn't mean to say I love you. He was just . . . he was just being Pete.

Passwords must be typed using the correct case, I thought.

I clicked OK and tried another: *ILOVEYOU.*

Blip.

I knew I knew. I wasn't going to reboot this computer this time. I would get it on the third try.

My dad once told me that the brain never forgets

anything. I closed my eyes and replayed the last time I spoke with my mother.

It was in her room at our apartment in Paris. We had just been to the Eiffel Tower. She had wrapped her arms around me and held me like I was a four-year-old. I stayed a long time and fell asleep.

Mom touched my cheek. I remembered exactly.

She said, "No matter where I am, I will always be in your heart." Then she said, "I love you," and she held up two fingers and said, "Together." Then she raised four fingers. "Forever."

On the laptop sitting on the dining room table, I typed the password: *Iloveyoutogetherforever*.

I was just about to tap the enter key, but my brain remembered the old password.

123Iamme.

Numbers. Numbers and letters.

I deleted the password and retyped.

Iloveyou2gether4ever.

And I hit enter.

 164

Open This First

The screen went blank for a second. Then a piano sound played as the desktop appeared.

I couldn't believe it. Or maybe I could.

"Yes! I got it!" I screamed at the top of my lungs. I jumped up and down so much that I almost knocked the computer off the table. I stared at the screen. I had done it. I had figured out Mom's password. I knew she had been sending me a sign. I didn't even really notice what was on the screen. I was too excited.

"I can't believe it. I did it!" I said, pumping my arms in the air.

Then I saw my name on the screen.

Sitting right there on the desktop were nine document files. Five of the nine files were the Explore the World stories. These were all that Mom was able to write. The next file was called "List of New Agents," the next two files read "For Calvert Only" and "For Uncle Paul," who was my mother's brother, and the title of the last document said "ELLIE Open this first."

A Letter

I double-clicked, and the document opened. It was a letter from my mom.

Dear Ellie,

How do I start such a letter? I don't really know. How about I think you're smart and beautiful and perfect! Since I am your mother, I might be a tad bit biased! :) That's just a little joke to get me started here.

I am writing this letter to you because I know you will eventually be the one to figure out my password.

Why did I change it?

I changed it because I think the stories are not ready to be read yet. The world will get through this spot it is in now, and later, maybe more people will be open to stories about other countries and cultures.

If you had the manuscripts too early, then I think you would rush to try to get them published, and you would get too many rejections, and the project would fail, again. The new password was my way to make you wait.

Now that you have figured out the code, I hope you try to find an agent only if you truly want to. But do it for yourself, and not for me. The reason I chose you was that your father will be in his own world. He will work, and that will make him feel better. It's his style. But, it will probably take him a long time to recover. He is a wonderful man, and I love him completely.

I thought about making a video, but I had trouble enough figuring out how to change the password on this computer, and I couldn't bear filming myself when I was bald. I guess I could have put Mandy on my head for a good laugh! I hope you threw that wig away. It was hideous, wasn't it? Thank you for sitting with me and telling me how pretty I was even when I wasn't.

Can I explain what happened? No. Can I tell you why I got ovarian cancer and not toe cancer? No, I can't. But I do know that the world isn't fair. Things are always out of balance. There will always be more water than land, and the water will not always be drinkable.

I want to tell you that today at the Eiffel Tower was so perfect. It was the best day of my life. Oh, I miss you already! I am not ready to leave. I never will be. I want to wake up tomorrow. I want it every day. I want it to keep going. I want to hold your father's hand one more time and walk with him after dinner, to run with him in the park again. Every day, I wake up, and I want to see you one more day. I would love to hug my mother and my father again.

Always and again, we want to say to the ones we love—just one more time—we want to whisper the three most powerful words on our planet, "I love you."

Know that I had fun in life, Ellie. That's what I want you to remember about me. Please take care of yourself. Be kind and keep your mind open. Think. Feel. Listen. And keep on the sunny side of life.

Iloveyou2gether4ever,
Mom

You Gave Me the Idea

I was strangely happy and sad at the same time. Once I stopped crying, I had to tell someone about the password.

Halfway across the park, I ran into Pete.

"I didn't mean to say what I said to you earlier," he said. "I mean that I—"

"Pete."

"Okay, okay. I'm quiet," he said. "Have you been crying? What's the matter?"

"Yes, I have been crying."

"Is everything all right?"

"Yeah." I nodded. "Everything's going to be just fine."

"Why are you smiling like that?"

"I figured out the password."

"What!" he said. "You got it open?"

I said, "And *you* gave me the idea."

"Me?"

"The password had 'I love you' in it."

"That's . . .," Pete bumbled. "That's awesome."

"Do you want to come to my house and open up the files of my mother's stories?"

"Your mom's Explore the World series?"

"All of them," I said.

"Wait!" he said like he had the best idea. "Let's have another party!"

"That's a great idea," I said. "Tomorrow after school, we'll have a book-reading party."

He pumped his arm. "Yes. And then we'll write letters to editors and get your mom's books published!"

Wait and See

The "I don't belong to a group" group showed up at my house promptly at three thirty the next afternoon.

Dad joined us this time. He had already printed out copies of each of the stories. So when Pete, Katie, Marcus, Gavin, Malia, and Hannah arrived, we were ready to read.

While we read, Dad called parents and teachers, telling them that we were working on a special, private, weeklong project. He told them that he would provide dinner and get them home by nine each night.

On the couches, in the chairs, on the floor, we read for hours without saying a word. Every now and then someone would catch a typo, and they would scribble in their manuscript.

Dad bought pizza, and each night we'd eat and read, and then Dad would take everyone home. At the end of the night I would send the day's corrections to my uncle, and he would do final edits. This happened for four days and nights straight.

Saturday was strategy day.

I didn't need to do much. The group was fired up,

and Pete started us off. "I think we ought to copy the books and send them to every single publisher in New York!"

"In the whole world," Marcus said.

Pete said, "Yeah!"

"That's too much," Hannah said. "I read a whole bunch of agents' websites last night, and what I've learned is that they want a query letter and a few sample chapters."

"A what?" Malia said, asking the question for everyone else.

Hannah was so professional. She explained that the query letter is sent out to promote the story in a few short lines, and then the agents send letters back if they are interested in the full manuscript.

"That sounds right to me," I said.

"Only a few chapters?" Pete asked. "You wouldn't get to the creepy catacombs section."

"Yeah," Katie said. "These stories are great."

"That's stupid," Marcus said. "You've got to send them a letter first and part of the book? And then they send you a letter back, and then you send them the whole book?"

Gavin shook his head and his hair flapped in his face. "It should be cloud-based anyway."

"Sounds like a waste of time," Malia said.

"I think," Hannah said, "the main reason is to get a sense of the writer's ability, their style."

"Why don't they just read the story?" Marcus said.

Hannah stayed cool. "Agents get more than a hundred letters a day from writers. So you have to go slowly. That's just the way it is."

"You could publish independently," Gavin said. "I used an indie publisher to help me publish two coding books of my own on the Kindle."

"Are you serious?" I asked. "We're still kids."

"It doesn't matter when you start doing grown-up things," Gavin said. "Kids are just pre-grown-ups, anyway."

"Kindle's a great idea," Hannah said. "But, let's try regular book publishing first. Okay?"

"What's regular book publishing?" Pete asked.

Hannah explained. "What I mean is, let's find a publisher with editors and designers, and they'll make it better and put it in book form and send it to all the bookstores."

We all nodded in unison. Hannah was right.

Dad cut through the living room, carrying empty pizza boxes. "Does anyone want breakfast?"

No one said anything.

"I just bought bacon and sausage and pancake mix," he said. "But I'll have to warn you. You can ask Ellie—I'm not the best cook in the world."

"I got it, sir," Marcus said. "I'm a chef."

"I've heard," Dad said.

"I'll help," Pete said.

"Me too," Gavin said.

While the boys made breakfast, the rest of us

listened to Hannah's plan.

"This is what I've learned," Hannah announced. "We have a list of ninety-nine literary agents. To each one, we will send a formal, professional email with a synopsis, and we'll put the first thirty pages of the manuscript in the email. That way there's no attachment; the story will be right there."

"How do you know all this?" I asked.

"Research."

Katie said, "I still don't understand why you only send thirty pages."

"In thirty pages you have a pretty good idea if you like a book or not," Hannah said. "And, this is perfect for us since on page twenty-nine is that hilarious diaper scene!"

We cracked up just thinking about it.

"Second," Hannah continued, "each one of us is going to add a one-line review. It's a children's book, so kids should be writing the reviews."

I liked the way Hannah thought. It was a brilliant plan.

After breakfast we drafted the best query letter ever. And sent it and thirty pages and our kid reviews to ninety-nine agents and editors in New York, London, Paris, Hong Kong, and Sydney. And for the last one, I took a chance and sent the whole series to an indie publisher.

Now it was time to wait and see.

 174

A Call

The first email came a couple of weeks later.

> *Dear Author,*
> *We apologize for responding in such an informal way with a form email letter, but . . . blah blah blah . . .*

The next email rejection said, *We do not take new authors without . . .*

And another: *Thank you for your submission, which I have carefully reviewed but must decline.*

A few days later an email from some guy in New York said, *We will only consider work from authors with a previously published writing history.*

I had talked with Mom about this same thing! So if you don't have something already published, then how do you get something published in the first place?

The next week we got four more email rejections and three rejections by regular mail.

By the end of February we had fifteen rejections in all. By mid-March, six weeks after sending out the letters, I decided to count up the rejections.

Eighty-three. It was terrible.

It was over, and I quit opening the emails.

On the first day of spring it was raining, and Dad was going to take me to school. While I was waiting for him, I looked at my email account. Eleven unopened emails. Ninety-four rejections in all. I immediately slapped the lid on the laptop closed, and I put my head down.

On the table right next to my ear, Dad's cell phone buzzed.

Dad was still in the shower, and I glanced at the caller ID. It read SEATTLE, WA.

It rang a third time, and I decided to answer it.

"Hello?"

"Good morning," said a man's voice. "Excuse me. I'm looking for Mr. Calvert Kerr or the daughter of Mrs. Etta Kerr."

"I'm h-her," I stuttered. "I mean, this is she. This is Ellie."

"Hello, Ellie," he said. "Are you also Ella?"

"Yes, I am."

"My name is Jack and I am an independent publisher. Did you by chance send us a letter and a series called Explore the World?"

"Yes."

"And these stories were written by your mother? Is that right?"

"Yes."

"It's my understanding that your mother . . . that your mom passed away last year? Is that correct?"

"Yes."

"I'm very sorry for your loss." He paused. "How old are you?"

"Twelve and three-quarters, today."

"Exactly twelve and three-quarters?"

"Yes."

He said, "I like math too." Then he paused. "I can't imagine how difficult something like that must be, especially at your age."

"Yeah, it is."

"Well, I'm sure your mother would be very proud of you."

"Thanks."

"In your letter," he said, "there were several very positive reviews for this story. I trust this is your built-in fan club."

"You could call it that," I said. "We had a read-a-thon a couple of months ago, and everyone loved the books. I mean, manuscripts."

"That's good for marketing," he said. "I, too, liked what I've read of your mom's work, and we'd like to help you publish them."

"Really?"

"Really," he said. "First I'll need to talk business, specifically about how to get set up on our system. Is your father around?"

"Yeah, sure," I said. I covered the mouthpiece of

the phone and screamed, "DAD!"

Dad jogged into the room wearing only dress pants and a T-shirt. "Who is it?"

"Jack Somebody, in Seattle," I whispered. "I think he's an indie publisher. Doesn't matter. He wants to help us publish Mom's stories!"

Dad whispered, "Jack?" He took the phone. "Hello," he said. "This is Calvert Kerr."

I leaned into my dad and listened in. " . . . And my team and I are reaching out to you today about your wife's Explore the World project."

"Yes," Dad said.

"First of all," Jack said, "let me say that I'm terribly sorry to hear about your wife. I can't begin to imagine your loss."

"Thank you," Dad said. "It's been a long haul, and Ellie has been so strong."

"You must be very proud of her."

"I am," Dad said and winked at me.

"I read the Explore the World series that Ellie sent me," Jack said. "And I loved it, and we have a team to help you and Ellie publish the work."

"And what's the catch?" Dad said.

"No catch," Jack said. "We value creative thinkers like your wife *and* your daughter. I think this series has global potential. Not to mention, the story of Ellie's publishing debut is impressive in and of itself."

"We're cautious," Dad said. "We have just had a lot of rejections in the past."

"I understand," Jack said. "Let me speak with my team and I'll reach out to you tomorrow, and we'll go from there."

"Sounds good," Dad said.

The next day an email from Jack arrived.

Memorandum
To: Calvert Kerr, Ella (Ellie) Elizabeth Kerr
From: Jack
Re: Etta Kerr and the Explore the World Series

Calvert and Ellie:

It was a pleasure to have spoken with you both yesterday. All of us are thrilled with the Explore the World project. We're confident of its success.

As you already know, Etta Kerr was an excellent storyteller. We're anxious to upload all the documents so that we can have a book ready by summer. At the bottom of this email you'll find several links for you to begin uploading the manuscripts to our secure server. I already have an editor and designer to help make it perfect.

I will call you later today to see if everything is to your satisfaction.

The End Is the Beginning

The last day of school came, and I was ready for summer. Dad and I were in the kitchen; he was drinking his coffee, and I was sitting at the breakfast table, eating a bowl of cereal.

"I have a surprise for you," he said.

"Is the book ready?"

"Actually," he said, "I have several surprises."

"What do you mean?"

"First of all," Dad said, "you know that they rushed this project to get the book ready for summer."

"And . . ."

"Well," Dad said. "It's ready!"

I couldn't believe it!

"In fact," Dad said, "the publisher is coming here today."

"What?"

"He's coming with a few copies of the book, and he said that they not only had already received positive reviews from the British and French critics, but he also wanted to ask the members of the 'I don't belong to a group' group if he could use their reviews on the book cover."

"Dad, this is the best!" I said. "Wait until I tell Pete and the others."

"You're amazing," he said. "I'm so proud of you."

"Mom actually was the one who wrote the stories," I said.

"True," Dad said.

"She would love this."

"She would," Dad said. "Listen. The publisher wants to present the book at this morning's assembly."

"What do you mean?" I said. "At school? We've already had our end-of-the-year assembly."

"Well," he said. "It is a book for kids, so we've actually planned a special meeting with Ms. Bean just to present the book."

"With Ms. Bean?"

Dad said, "She's just tired. She's retiring this year."

"I know," I said. "We had a whole assembly about it last week. It was awful. She cried."

"Ms. Bean is retiring for personal reasons."

"What does that mean?"

"Sometimes," Dad said, "when people retire for personal reasons, it can mean they have an illness they don't want to talk about."

"Maybe being sick made her a little grouchy."

"Maybe," Dad said. "But she's been very helpful to me, and she's happy to do an assembly for *us*."

"Why did you say *us* like that?"

"That's the other surprise," he said. "Guess who's providing the music for the assembly?"

181

"I don't know," I said. "Who's playing?"

"Antoine."

"You mean *Antoine* Antoine? From France?"

"Yes, his jazz band is playing at a festival this summer in San Francisco. So I asked him to come a few weeks early."

Dad washed out his coffee cup. He had a look like he was still hiding something.

"What else, Dad?"

"Just wait," he said with a smirk.

A car horn blew in the driveway.

"Who's here?" I asked.

Dad said nothing. I ran out the front door, leaping over the old welcome mat. I saw her getting out of the back seat.

"Munda!" I screamed.

I nearly knocked her over, jumping up into her arms. She dropped her tiny suitcase. Then she spun me around and set me back down, her hands resting on my shoulders.

"My little coconut tree," she said. "Look at you now. You going to grow to the sky. Oh my Lord."

I jumped up again and hugged her. "What are you doing here?"

"I am coming to get my medical degree."

"I thought you were going to school in France?"

"I had a better offer."

"So you're going to go to school here?"

"I am," she said. "With the help of my friends."

She looked toward my dad, who was now standing in the doorway.

I said, "You told me that medical school was expensive."

"Munda took care of us," Dad said, "and it's time to pay her back."

Munda, Dad, and I walked into the school gym. Onstage there was a three-piece band: piano, drums, and Antoine on the cello. They were playing a happy jazz tune. Ms. Hart and Jack, the publisher, met us at the door, and we all shook hands.

The inside of the gym was packed with rows and rows of kids sitting in chairs on what was normally our basketball court. The hoops and backboards were pulled up to the ceiling.

Munda, Dad, and I walked down the center aisle and sat in the front row with Jack. Sitting right behind us in the second row was my group.

Ms. Bean stood at the microphone in front of Antoine's band.

"Children," she said, clapping her hands together. "Calm down. Now even though today is the last day of school, I still expect your behavior to conform to the guidelines of school policy. This is a special assembly to introduce an exceptional project to the world.

"We are thrilled to be here today. Now, as most of you already know, Ellie Kerr took it upon herself to locate her late mother's stories and shepherd them through to publication. No doubt a daunting task. We here at the Grassland School could not be more proud of you, Miss Ellie. Congratulations!"

There was a big round of applause, and for the first time I actually kind of liked Ms. Bean. I looked up at her clapping onstage, and she smiled and winked at me.

"Before I tear up like at the last assembly," Ms. Bean said, "I am going to turn the microphone over to the band."

Antoine took the microphone from Ms. Bean, and we clapped a little, while Jack walked up the steps and stood on the side of the stage.

"Ladies and gentlemen, *mesdames et messieurs*," Antoine said in his thick French accent. "Not too many French people here I guess."

The two French teachers laughed.

"I am pleased to be here," he said. "Firstly, I was a friend of Ellie's mother. She was a wonderful person full of sunshine and happiness. I miss her, and I am happy to know that her stories will soon be out in the world."

Everyone clapped lightly.

Antoine continued. "I want to thank Ellie and Mr. Calvert Kerr for making this possible. I know them from when they lived in France. I would like to say that Ellie is incredibly courageous. You are all lucky to have her as a friend and a student in your school."

The whole assembly cheered.

Antoine spoke into the microphone, and a hush fell over the crowd. "I would like to introduce the publisher of Ellie's mother's stories. Please give a big applause for Monsieur Jack!"

Everyone clapped again while the publisher went onstage and took the microphone. He was bald with a big smile and wearing a blue jacket.

"Thank you very much," Jack said. "A special thank you to the Grassland School for putting this assembly together on such short notice. So without further ado, I would like to present a project that my company has been working on."

A few people whistled.

"First, I would like to say a few words about an extraordinarily daring and bold student. Intrepid, I would call her. You all know Ellie Kerr, but I want you to know that she has fought an uphill battle in a business that is rarely nice to even the thickest-skinned writers out there. Ellie's mother, Etta Kerr, wrote wonderful stories yet died tragically before anyone ever took note. But this young woman was undeterred in seeing that her mother's stories were published. With the help of her father and uncle and a few friends, Ellie was able to unlock the treasure trove of stories that will enrich our lives for many years to come. And second, she has been able to navigate this labyrinth we call publishing. Without further ado, please give a big round of applause to"—Jack pointed to me—"Miss Ellie Kerr."

Everyone in the whole school started clapping. I put my hands together too but I was clapping for my mom. She wrote the stories.

Pete, who was right behind me, nudged me up onto the platform with Antoine and Jack. The stage lights, blue and red, were shining in my eyes. That's when I noticed the TV crews in the back of the auditorium. There were cameras and reporters with microphones. There was ABC and the British station, the BBC, and even CANAL TV from France was there. This was no regular school assembly. This was my father's doing. He couldn't hang a painting on the wall, but he knew a thing or two about marketing and business. Antoine stroked the strings of his cello once again to quiet everyone down.

Jack then handed me a copy of Mom's book. There it was. In black and white. A book, not a manuscript.

I thought, *Mom, you did it.*

"Everyone," Jack said. "I'd like to present to you today for the first time, the first book in the Explore the World series!"

Antoine played music, and everyone stood up and clapped. I held the book up over my head like it was a trophy. In my heart, I could feel Mom. I smiled so big!

It turns out there *is* a first time for everything. It wasn't the first time a book was published

 186

posthumously, but it was the first time for my mom.

For me? Oh, this book was the first of many to come. *Definitely!*

Ellie

A Note from Paul Aertker

One of my beta readers said to me, "I'm curious. What inspired you to tackle this subject?"

I think it was because of my friend, Chris, who died way too young. He, like Etta, had a beautiful sense of humor and generosity during his illness. I still think about him a lot.

And what's more, this is a story that very much feels it was told to me. So I'm really just passing it along.

Paul Aertker

Paul Aertker (ETT-Kerr) is a children's book writer, teacher, and frequent speaker at elementary and middle schools. He began his teaching career in West Africa with the Peace Corps where he helped establish the town's first public library. His first series, Crime Travelers, consistently ranks in the top spot in multiple categories. The series has been optioned for TV and Film. He and his wife live inColorado and travel with their two children whenever possible.

More information at paulaertker.com

Made in the USA
Middletown, DE
18 April 2019